House Doctor

Instant Makeovers

My thanks go to the following people: My co-author Fanny Blake, Katie Cowan, Barbara Saulini, Emma Dickens and all at Essential Books, my agent Cat Ledger, Myles Archibald and Angela Newton at Harper Collins. Thanks again to the fabulous Production and Makeover personnel at Talkback Productions and to Channel 5 Publicity who have worked tirelessly to make yet another successful series. Special thanks to all the contributors who opened their doors to me and the House Doctor team. And finally, thank you to my dear family and friends in America for their undying support and understanding during my many absences.

First published in Great Britain in 2002 by
HarperCollins*Publishers*
77–85 Fulham Palace Road
London W6 8JB
www.**fire**and**water**.com

Design: Barbara Saulini for Essential Books
Editorial: Emma Dickens for Essential Books

www.housedoctor.co.uk

57910864

Printed and bound in Great Britain by Bath Press Ltd

A catalogue record for this book is available from the British Library

ISBN: 0-00-714425-3

House Doctor

Instant Makeovers

Ann Maurice
with Fanny Blake

CONTENTS

INTRODUCTION

It's difficult to believe that a year has gone by since my second book *House Doctor Quick Fixes* was published. I want to thank you all for your continued interest and support, without which this third book would not have been possible. I am thrilled to bring you *Instant Makeovers* because not only does it include case studies from last year's series, but it goes a step further. In my opinion, it is my best book yet!

what's the book about?

I have expanded the scope of this book to include tips on how to maintain and improve one's home as well as one's lifestyle. Much of the information in this book can be used by anyone whether selling their property or not. There are 'How to' sections filled with information on painting and decorating; revamping furniture, wooden floors and tired-looking rooms; and tips on creating a focal point, the art of display and disguising an unpleasant view. It shows you how to make the most of your lighting and window treatments, and even how to use plants to enhance your interior.

Finally, I have also included a series of 'hands on' step-by-step projects that turn theory into practice. These 'tricks of the trade' are well illustrated and show what can be achieved with minimum effort for maximum effect. They are meant to be done at home in a day or two by anyone with little or no DIY or decorating experience. Most importantly, they are meant to be fun. I sincerely hope that all of you will 'have a go'.

selling your home

Meanwhile, the *House Doctor* television series continues to be a smashing success – I guess the British viewing public has not yet tired of hearing me bang on and on about clutter, doggie odour and garish paint colours. We are currently in our fifth year of programming and, by the time we have completed this year, I will have filmed a total of 59 original episodes, in 59 real people's homes across the whole of Britain. Phew!

Getting the highest and best price for your home is not rocket science. Based on my years of experience as an estate agent, as well as an interior designer, I have devised a systematic approach to preparing homes for the market that really works. However, there are several key ingredients that are necessary for it to be a success. These are:

- commitment
- detachment
- cooperation

COMMITMENT

Commitment is the first key ingredient. Unless someone is truly committed to selling their home, mentally and emotionally prepared to move on, they will not take all the necessary steps along the path to getting it sold. Be clear on the result that you want to achieve before beginning what can be the stressful process of selling and moving house.

DETACHMENT

The second key ingredient is detachment. You need to be able to step back and view your home through 'buyers' eyes', with your vision not clouded by personality, memories or emotion. This is the point at which I have to remind prospective sellers of this crucial mental nuance: 'You are not selling your home, you are selling a house.' An impersonal and objective attitude is necessary in order to achieve the desired result.

COOPERATION

The third key ingredient is cooperation. Unless there is the cooperation and involvement of all household members, the task at hand will be extremely daunting. Everyone involved needs to be 'on the same page' in order to make it work. It must be the case of all energies on board, moving towards the same goal – the sale.

metaphor of the self

One would think, then, that sooner or later the British viewing public would get wise to the notion that what I have been preaching works. You would think, moreover, that more and more people would be aware that proper presentation of their properties would not only lead to a quick sale, but also get a higher price. So why, then, are there still homes being put up for sale that are unkempt, cluttered, dirty and poorly presented?

This is not just my hyper-critical eye, nor my skewed 'American' perspective. For I receive loads of mail from people in this country, and am even stopped on the street by people asking such questions as: 'How can people live like this?' 'How could anyone possibly try and sell their house in such a state?' Better yet: 'How can they not see in their own homes what the viewers see?' Well, the answer is simple. It's called *denial*.

Let me explain. You've heard me say that 'the home is the metaphor of the self'. This means that the state of one's inner self is reflected in the state of one's home. That is why clearing away of clutter and reorganising of belongings can effect a change in one's life. It allows a person to become 'unstuck' and able to move on. When I first visit a house, I must quickly determine why it has not sold. First I have a look at the space itself and define the problem areas. These are the things that viewers have come to be familiar with many times over throughout the programmes, such as clutter, bold colours, shabby conditions and bad furniture placement. Then I determine the corrections that have to be made in order to set the property right. This is the easy part.

What might not be completely obvious is that I then need to determine the psychological issues surrounding the homeowners' situation that allow them to 'pretend' to be selling their homes, without ever actually achieving a sale. This is where things get somewhat more complicated. You see, even though people convince themselves consciously that they want to move, more often than not in these extreme cases, there are underlying issues that exist on a subconscious level that stand in their way. These are usually based on fear of change and are manifested in various scenarios.

Here are some of the most common issues:

- Living in the past: The house holds memories – a family home where children have moved on, a once happy marriage that has collapsed, a spouse who has passed on.
- Loss of fortune: Due to unfortunate personal or financial circumstances, selling the house would mean a step down in terms of status.
- Punishment of a spouse or partner: The house needs to be sold as part of a divorce settlement or because of a job transfer, creating underlying resentment and resistance.
- Loss of control: These people can't bear rocking the boat. It would be too chaotic.
- Lack of support systems: This is common with those living on their own. They just can't seem to do it without another's help.
- Arrogance: These people think that their house is wonderful exactly the way it is and that anyone else who doesn't see it the same way is just ignorant.
- Fear: These people have no plan and so have nothing to look forward to.
- Greed: Their house is worth less than the figure they are asking for it.
- Laziness: People will come up with hundreds of excuses, none of which holds water.

You've seen such people on the programme. These people surround themselves with clutter, dirt, unfinished DIY jobs and overgrown gardens. They make excuses such as lack of time or money; they blame others – their spouses, children, even their estate agents! And in so doing they never have to take that big scary step called moving.

So while the *House Doctor* team goes about making changes to the house, I spend time helping these people see why their home hasn't sold. It is an amazing process to watch. As their home becomes decluttered and depersonalised, they begin to detach themselves from it. Often they get upset, even angry at first. This is a natural part of 'letting go'. Then gradually as they become more and more involved, they begin to wonder how they could have let things go for so long. Finally there comes a turning point when they actually see and appreciate the result of all our efforts. Although it looks a thousand times better, it no longer feels like their home. In fact, they feel slightly uncomfortable there. They have finally made the mental and emotional break. They are ready to sell. They begin talking about moving on in a positive manner, begin visualising their future. The House Doctor's task is complete.

Ann Maurice   (www.housedoctor.co.uk)

BECKENHAM

1930s-style detached family house with four bedrooms, two reception rooms, kitchen, bathroom, 80ft garden. In need of some modernisation and decoration. £349,995.

Beckenham is a quiet suburban town, only a 20-minute train ride from London and another 20 minutes from the M25 and escape to the Kentish countryside. Lying within the borough of Bromley, Beckenham boasts a good number of parks and public spaces and has its own river, the Beck, running through its centre. Its thriving high street contains numerous restaurants, bars and shops and there are two theatres, a cinema, tennis club and leisure centre for those who enjoy the arts and sport. Wide tree-lined residential roads contain a great range of property styles, from modern apartment blocks and conversions to period semi-detached and detached houses. Because of its amenities and excellent transport links, this is a particularly desirable area where properties are normally pounced on the moment they come on the market.

Robert and his wife Gillian, a retired jazz singer, had decided to sell up now their two daughters had left home: 'It's been a lovely home for the last twenty years, but now we want to move.' But easier said than done. Despite being a desirable, large, detached house with four bedrooms and sizeable garden, it had been on the market for fourteen months without a bite and in the meantime Robert and Gillian had missed out on a couple of houses they would have liked to have made an offer on themselves.

There wasn't a lot wrong with the house but it was easy to see what could be done to make it look more attractive. It must have looked great when they moved in all those years ago, but not much had been done to the house since and it showed. The colours and furnishings made the house look as though it had been lost in a time warp – especially the quaint living-room suite and the banisters in the hall. The rooms were crowded with bits and pieces that had been accumulated over the years as the family grew up. But, sadly, where Robert and Gillian saw family treasures, any potential buyer would see clutter. It was no good Robert hoping for a buyer with imagination to save the day. Why wait for that rare bird? He could make a sale happen faster by removing any distractions, so that anyone stepping through the front door could immediately imagine themselves living there. If he wanted someone else to do up the house, then that should have been reflected in the asking price. I decided to leave the upstairs rooms as they were and focus on the ground floor because first impressions are so important.

Doctor's Diagnosis

To make it grab the buyer we had to:
- Restore the original parquet floors
- Redecorate in today's colours
- Declutter
- Hire a new living-room suite

BEFORE
viewers' comments

'The outside looks nice but the inside needs so much work. Is it worth the effort and the money?'

'It's so dated. You'd have to spend £40 – 45,000 modernising it to your requirements.'

'The hallway's a bit cluttered. It's more like a workroom.'

'The kitchen's terrible. That would cost at least another £5,000 to do up.'

AFTER

entrance

The entrance hall is crucial for establishing positive initial reactions. It sets the tone for the rest of the house. As it was, this entrance looked more like a workroom than a welcome. An upright piano stood in one corner, the carpet was dated, the banisters were straight out of the 1960s and the area was very cluttered. It was time to redefine and renovate. First of all the piano had to be found another home. Then it was up with the carpet to reveal the original parquet floor. We revitalised it by vigorously cleaning with one part turpentine, one part vinegar and one part methylated spirits, then waxing. A Persian rug added colour and warmth to the space, as well as dividing it so that the work space was notionally separate. I had an idea for using the banisters somewhere else, so replaced them with traditional spindles and a handrail more in keeping with the period of the house. They come in kit form and although not difficult to put up, it can be worth getting in a professional to be sure of getting them straight.

The walls were painted a light bright neutral colour and I added some simple curtains that wouldn't detract from the hall itself. I also replaced the light fittings, which had seen better days, with discreet wall uplighters. Then it was time to dress the space. I tidied the desk and installed an occasional table and a mirrored coat stand which clearly defined the space. The finishing touches were fresh flowers and a potted plant to add a bit of life. The result was elegant but warm and friendly.

Gillian
The hall and stairway are particularly special because they make a light and wonderfully spacious entrance to the house

living

This room definitely lacked the 'wow' factor and needed a radical overhaul. The first thing I noticed was the evidence of Gillian's love of reading. There were books everywhere. Some of them would have to be found a new home so that the room could be shown off at its most spacious. Ten box-loads later, I was able to make a feature of the box shelves using them to display ornaments as well as books. Being able to see the depth of the shelves does help add to the sense of space. The room lacked a strong focal point but the solution was found by unblocking the original fireplace and stone hearth. To play it up, we painted the brickwork white, recycled part of the hall banister as a mantelpiece, found a new hearth and grate at a local salvage yard and hung a large mirror above. Sadly, a local chimney sweep recommended we didn't light a fire but even without it, a strong decorative feature had been established. The dated colour scheme of green and grey did nothing but deaden the atmosphere. Instead I chose a smock flat matt emulsion for the walls. The carpet, which had seen years of use, was replaced by a new one in a more neutral shade to give a plush, luxurious feel. The view of the garden was hidden by my pet hate – net curtains. I took them down and hung new cream curtains to frame the view without detracting from it. Then it was time to say goodbye to the very dated but

AFTER

comfortable three-piece suite. Robert and Gillian didn't want to get rid of it altogether so they put it into storage for their next home while I hired a sophisticated cream suite which altogether transformed the room. Hiring furniture is something that is frequently done in America and there are a number of companies that will do it in the UK. It's a route well worth considering if you need extra furniture when staging your home for a quick sale. When we'd finished, we had a sophisticated room much more likely to appeal to today's buyers.

BEFORE

dining

Perhaps because it was used less than the other rooms in the house, the dining room had accumulated most of Robert and Gillian's treasures. They had recently

AFTER

returned from India, having vowed and failed not to bring home any more souvenirs. And here they were. What the couple needed to do was to thin out their belongings and reorganise some key items. The bookcase was removed and the dresser moved to another wall, liberating a space for the piano in one of the alcoves and leaving the other empty so that a couple of pictures and a small table could be featured. Robert and Gillian had collected all sorts of china on the dresser. I asked them to remove everything then to put back just a few of the best pieces. The original parquet floor hidden under the worn carpet was in excellent condition and just needed treating in the same way as the hall floor. The wallpaper was painted cream, the net curtains were removed and, to lighten the sofa in the window, I added some aquamarine cushions to coordinate with the table runner and chairs, bringing the room together. Robert is a keen painter and my favourite finishing touch was to give pride of place over the fireplace to one of his earliest paintings.

AFTER

kitchen

The last room on the list really let the house down. The oak units may once have been fashionable but now looked heavy and dated, adding to the gloomy atmosphere in the cramped, unhappy kitchen. The kitchen is one of the major selling points in a house so must look as light, bright, clean and friendly as possible. If it looks as if it needs replacing, buyers will immediately be wondering where they're going to find the extra £20,000 or so that it will cost for a new one. The chances are they'll prefer to

AFTER

find another house altogether. Somehow,
I had to make this room look more up to
the minute.

First of all I wanted to hide the unsightly
boiler so had it boxed in with MDF to
streamline the surfaces. The walls were
brightened up with a coat of mellow sage. It
was far too expensive to replace the units but
painting them in cream gloss and replacing
the handles with something more modern
immediately gave them a new lease of life.
The combination of the new colours gave the
room a much-needed sense of space. This
was reinforced by the removal of the
decorative plates from the walls and by
replacing the enormous breakfast table with

a neat breakfast bar for two. Curtains rarely do much for a kitchen. They tend to attract dust and get in the way. Almost hidden behind the existing ones was a discreet roller blind which, on its own, provided a more modern look.

I know Robert found the whole process particularly painful. He would have liked to hang on to everything in the house. This is completely understandable, considering it had been their family home for so long and contained so many happy mementoes. But if the property was to sell, they had to make the interior more sophisticated and stylish to appeal to today's buyers, most of whom want to be able to move in without having to undertake massive renovation and redecoration. By the time the last accessory was put in place, both he and Gillian appreciated what I was trying to achieve and felt confident they would be moving soon. Sure enough, they did.

> ' Robert
> The choice of colours and the new materials made me realise just how dated the old furnishings were

COST	
Paint	£200
Carpet	£650
Furniture hire	£530

'Abingdon suite,The Roomservice Furnishing Group, £530 per month
'Windsor' stair parts, £220 Richard Burbidge

Accessories	£690

including 'Zang' breakfast bar, MFI, £149

Labour	£400
TOTAL	£2,690

AFTER
viewers' comments

'You don't walk in and see everything you'll have to do. It's been done.'

'A total transformation.'

'It's got everything you look for in a house. It's a place to relax.'

how to

REVAMP YOUR KITCHEN / BATHROOM

If either your kitchen or your bathroom has lost its sparkle, it doesn't mean you have to spend a fortune buying a new one. Assess the room. If the worktops, flooring, appliances or fittings are exhausted then replace them. Thoroughly cleaning all the surfaces will make the biggest difference. Empty cupboards and throw away anything that you don't need, making room for all the junk that has accumulated on the work surfaces. If there are any DIY jobs left undone, now is the time to fix them. Handles and switches should be properly screwed in and cleaned.

floors

Old, stained and worn carpets should go straight to the tip. There is a huge choice of different floorcoverings available that are easy to lay, easy to clean and easy on the pocket. Timber floors are suitable for both kitchens and bathrooms only if they are treated properly. In a kitchen, bits of food and dirt will get between the joins while in a bathroom there is a danger that water may seep through and rot the wood. Wood-effect floors are easy to fit and are a smart alternative for the kitchen. Otherwise, it's worth considering vinyl or linoleum (in tile or sheet form), made in a wide variety of designs and patterns, or cork tiles. For a bathroom, vinyl and linoleum are always good solutions but you might also consider rubber (in tile or sheet form).

walls

A coat or two of paint can magically transform your kitchen or bathroom into a totally different environment. Kitchens can take a variety of colour schemes. They are the heart of the home and will respond well to cheery combinations of colours. To keep the mood of a bathroom intimate and relaxing, use pale, calming colours. Both rooms can be painted in an eggshell or vinyl finish. These paints are practical in a kitchen where they can easily be wiped clean, and are ideal in a bathroom because they are waterproof.

tiles

Tiles provide a hygienic, hard-wearing surface that is ideal for both kitchens and bathrooms. However, to look their best, they must be kept spotless. If cleaning them isn't enough to spruce up the room, there are a number of ways to improve their look without necessarily going to the trouble of replacing them. First inspect the grouting. If it has been painted, you may want to change the colour by using specialist grout-painting pens. Always do a test area first and see how it reacts over a couple of weeks. Alternatively, get rid of any discoloured or cracked areas by carefully regrouting. This will involve removing the existing grout, then applying and levelling new grout (specialist tools are available in DIY shops for both these jobs). Use a damp cloth to wipe off the excess. It may also be necessary to reseal the join between the tiles and the bathtub by cutting out the old sealant and applying new. If the tiles themselves are stained, dated, the wrong colour or just plain ugly, there are a number of specialist tile paints that will instantly transform them. Alternatively, you may want to give them a new lease of life by sticking on small ceramic or vinyl appliqués, such as ceramic shells or pots of herbs.

windows

Clear window ledges of all but one or two decorative items. Clean the windows until they shine. Curtains are not always practical in either a kitchen or bathroom. Blinds offer a neat uncluttered look and are relatively inexpensive. They can be rolled back out of the way and they can be waterproof in the bathroom and wipeable in the kitchen. They can introduce colour and pattern, are inexpensive and can be easily replaced. You may be able to find ready-made blinds that fit, you may want to use a DIY blind kit or, of course, you can have them made to measure.

lighting

Lighting can make a huge difference to the perception of a room. It is important that the kitchen work surfaces, hob and oven are all lit efficiently. Fluorescent lighting strips can run under the upper kitchen cabinets to prevent the cook having to work in his or her own shadow. Alternatively, light can be directed from the ceiling, either from a track carrying spotlights or from accurately angled downlighters. If the kitchen includes a dining area, it's a good idea to install dimmer switches so that the work areas can be faded out during a meal.

   Bathroom lighting is strictly regulated to avoid water coming in contact with it. The only switch acceptable in the room is a pull cord. Otherwise switches should be mounted outside the room. Dimmer switches enable you to change the mood in your bathroom, creating a more soothing atmosphere in the evenings. In addition to overhead lighting there should be lighting above or on either side of the mirror. Fluorescent lights are particularly unflattering. The basin/shaving area might have a shaving light socket. To create an intimate, relaxing mood, have scented candles around the bath. Their light will also have the advantage of disguising any real eyesores.

kitchen units

Kitchen units can make or break the look of a kitchen. Dark wooden doors can be overpowering and dated. Melamine finishes may look as if they have seen better days. One of the easiest ways of getting a new kitchen at a fraction of the price is by replacing the doors and drawer fronts. Most replacement door manufacturers sell them in MDF, hardwood and pine.

If you want a new look without going to such measures, try painting the existing units. First, they must be spotlessly clean, then just sand them enough for the primer to stick. Prime then apply the topcoat. Melamine cupboards and drawers can be painted with specialist melamine paint. If the units have a dated wood surround, just painting it may be enough to bring your kitchen smartly into the 21st century. Changing the handles is another simple trick to give a completely new look. Is there any way you can improve the look of your worktop without replacing it? Tiles can be regrouted or painted (see above). Wooden surfaces can be sanded, then re-oiled or resealed. Zinc and stainless steel tops can be cleaned with lemon juice to give an extra sheen.

bathroom suite

Do not use acid cleaners or abrasive cleaners or cloths to clean the bathroom fittings. They may remove the stains but they will also remove the surface glaze. A proprietary brand of limescale remover will get rid of any unsightly drip marks. Use it to clean around the openings of the taps and the plughole. Touch up enamel chips or badly marked baths with specialist enamel paint. It's quick to apply and gives a finish as good as new. Stop dripping taps by tightening or replacing the washer. Replace tatty shower curtains or watermarked shower doors, and invest in a new toilet seat.

UPDATED CHEST OF DRAWERS

Take years off a plain chest of drawers with a facelift that
brings it winging its way into the 21st century

What you need

- chest of
  drawers
- screwdriver
- tape measure
  and pencil
- saw or jigsaw
- 10mm (⅜in)
  MDF
- protective face
  mask
- panel pins and
  hammer
- PVA glue
- 15mm (⅝in)

- pine board
- 4 legs (in kit
  form)
- medium-grade
  sandpaper
- paintbrushes
- 2 shades of
  vinyl matt
  emulsion paint
- liquid beeswax
  and soft cloths
- clear resin
  knobs

1 Remove the handles from the
drawers. Turn the chest upside down
and measure its length and breadth.
Cut a piece of MDF, wearing a face
mask for protection, to fit and secure to
the base of the chest using panel pins
30mm (1¼in) apart. To fill out the
recessed panel, measure its width and
height, adding 10mm (⅜in) to cover
the new MDF. Cut the pine to measure
and stick in place with PVA glue.

2 Screw securing plates on the MDF base, 15mm (⅝in) from each corner. Screw in the new legs.

3 Remove the drawers. Sand them and the chest before painting with two coats of emulsion, using the darker shade for the body of the chest and alternating it with the lighter shade on the drawer fronts. When the paint is dry, wax the entire surface with beeswax. Buff till it gleams using a soft cloth. Add the new knobs to complete the look.

CLACTON-ON-SEA

Two-bedroom bungalow in
cul-de-sac with bright
living room, kitchen,
bathroom, sun lounge.
£69,995.

Seven miles of clean beaches are not the only entertainment in the classic English resort town of Clacton-on-Sea. It has one of the longest piers in the country and a promenade also providing plenty of amusements. Only a two-hour drive from London, Clacton offers plenty of sun, sea and sand. The residence of choice is the bungalow and there are plenty of them to choose from. These one-storey wonders are mostly irresistible and get snapped up quickly. But I was called in to rescue one of the pint-sized properties which had lost its appeal and had been on the market for an unbelievable seven months.

It was the home of ex-merchant seaman and chauffeur Billy and his partner Margaret. They had decided to sell up in order to go and live in America to be close to Margaret's family in New Jersey and Billy's nine-year-old son, Spencer, who lived with his mother in Oregon. Margaret thought she understood why people weren't keen to buy the house: 'It's not ready to move into. Billy pulled it apart when he moved in here. That's what's put people off.'

She had hit the nail on the head. I was shocked by the way they were presenting their home. It was no wonder no one was interested in buying it. From the moment of pulling up outside the house, my heart sank. The front garden was a mess with nothing much else but weeds growing in it. The outside of the house looked uninviting and didn't even have a working front door. The entrance was through the sun lounge into the kitchen. This, the first room I saw, was a shambles. Billy had begun all sorts of DIY jobs and had failed to finish any of them. He admitted he didn't like the way it looked but had never got round to doing anything about it. I had a feeling things could only get worse from there and I was right.

The bathroom was in a disgusting state and needed completely refitting and decorating. Spencer's bedroom was hideous. The camouflage décor was decidedly off-putting, not to mention the fact that the bed was in pieces against the wall. In the master bedroom, things weren't much better. The bed was unusually placed in the centre of the room so that Billy and Margaret could move around easily and get to the open shelves holding Billy's neatly organised and folded clothes. I had seen enough. When selling your house, you are selling its potential to a buyer. If the buyer can't see it, you've lost your sale. It was impossible to see past the clutter and botched or unfinished jobs. Something had to be done if they were ever to fulfil their dream of getting to America.

Doctor's Diagnosis

For the best presentation we had to:

- Give it kerb appeal
- Finish the DIY jobs
- Tidy the bedrooms
- Neutralise the living room

BEFORE
viewers' comments

'The garden's a bit of a wilderness.'

'This would have to be completely gutted.'

'I wouldn't want a bath in there.'

'You couldn't just move in. You'd have to pay more money for someone else to sort it all out.'

Margaret
It's not ready to move into. That's what's putting people off

AFTER

entrance

I started with the approach to the house. The way it looked at the moment, any buyer would be forgiven for driving off without coming in. The garden needed to be thoroughly weeded and replanted. In case Billy couldn't bring himself to keep up the weeding, we covered any exposed earth with gravel and pebbles to give it a seaside theme and keep the weeds down. Margaret gave the windows a good clean and now they stood a chance of hooking a buyer from the outset.

The next thing was to reinstate the front door and hallway. Signal the front door, once you have made sure the paintwork and door furniture are gleaming, by putting a couple of welcoming pot plants on either side of it. The hall had not been fulfilling its proper function as an entrance to the home and had become dark and neglected as a result. We moved the coats out of the way so the passage was clear, then gave it a completely new floor. Self-adhesive wood effect strips stick easily on to a clean surface and give a bright, hard-wearing finish. Finally, painting the walls a light neutral shade and hanging some clip-framed art completed its transformation into an entrance that invited you into the rest of the house.

BEFORE

Spencer's bedroom

First on my hit list was Spencer's room. Once we had emptied it, I could see where to begin if a buyer was to see the potential of the room. Fortunately, we didn't have Spencer to contend with as Billy painted over the camouflaged walls. 'This is my favourite room,' he pointed out, wistfully. 'But I know he'll understand because it will help me move on and be closer to him.'

I decided on a seaside theme, so the walls were painted blue and I used accessories such as a lifebelt and some bright plastic buckets on one shelf and tiny coloured beach huts on another. Billy finally built the bed and put it next to the wall. A jaunty red-striped duvet cover chimed with the carpet and curtains, both of which were already in the room but barely noticeable under the chaos. As a nod to the family's army connections, I allowed an orderly row of toy soldiers back on to a shelf but now they looked a little upgraded given their new surroundings. I decided to take the computer from the living room and give it pride of place in a corner. The room now clearly gave the message that it could be used as a small second bedroom or even as an office.

AFTER

master bedroom

In the case of the master bedroom, it was enough to work with what was already there. First of all, the shelves and clothes were firmly removed from view. Immediately, the room looked bigger. The walls were painted a gorgeous peach to tone with the red carpet and curtains. I didn't want the room to look too masculine so we bought a matching duvet and curtains with a pretty sprigged print. The curtains looked great tied back above the original red ones and framed the window magnificently. Then all that

BEFORE

was required was to rearrange the furniture to make the most of the space. With the bed against the wall, there was room for the white chest of drawers to double as a bedside table. I put the pine chest at the foot of the bed, having rejuvenated it with a coat of 50 per cent water/50 per cent emulsion. The remaining shelf looked better displaying four atmospheric candles than Billy's old jumpers. The new look was tied together with the red accents in the cushions, the curtains and the picture over the bed. A few simple measures proved enough to make the room light, bright, welcoming and fresh.

AFTER

bathroom

Words almost failed me when I first saw the bathroom. It was one of the worst I have ever seen in my career. Nobody would be able to imagine themselves relaxing in a grimy bath tub with a hole in it, in the midst of a building site. Drastic action was required. All the bathroom fittings had to be replaced. Billy invested in a shell-like design that echoed the seaside theme in Spencer's bedroom. After boxing in the bath and the exposed pipework we ripped off the existing wallpaper and reapplied a more subtle paper with a difference: the adhesive was applied to the walls, not the paper, and the paper was stuck on, remembering to leave a little extra top and bottom so it could be cut to a perfect fit. We tore up the remnants of the black and white flooring and laid marble-effect tiles. The grubby shower curtain made way for a new and stylish one in aqua and the room was furnished with a large mirror over the basin and new soap and towels. With everything spotlessly clean and tidy, it was unrecognisable as the same room.

AFTER

BEFORE

kitchen

When I first visited the house, the kitchen was the first room any buyer came to and it was a complete tip. Emergency surgery was the only option. Having prepared the walls and plastered over the exposed wires, Billy painted them a soft, neutral green which I'd mixed using a beige paint with some green emulsion stainer. It looked great. It covered the marks left by the

AFTER

wall units that Billy had pulled down because 'they were winding me up'. Carpet is always a mistake in a kitchen and this tatty green one was no exception. It made way for the same easy-to-lay and easy-to-clean vinyl flooring that we used in the hall. The boiler door was found in the attic (where else?), brought downstairs and put in its rightful place. Painting the units white gave them a whole new lease of life, as did a thorough clean for everything else. All that remained were the old tricks of selecting one or two items to grace the worktop, some toning tea towels and fresh herbs and flowers on the window ledge. It looked as good as new.

living

With the reinstatement of the front door, the living room was the final room the buyer would enter so it needed to confirm everything she or he had thought about the bungalow so far. The lurid yellow walls would not be to everyone's taste so they were repainted a softer shade. The room looked more spacious with the furniture rearranged

AFTER

so the sitting area was concentrated around a coffee table by the window. Without the garish red drape, the sofa looked much more discreet and stylish. Then I added a small dining table in the area by the door, framing it with the two green chairs and positioning a shelf and a peaceful picture above it. We took down the untidy shelves, hung some sheer curtains at the windows and added a surround and mantel to the fireplace to give it a more traditional feel. It didn't take much to transform it into a restful haven.

Although we sometimes had to drag Billy back from sunbathing to the job in hand, both he and Margaret were convinced by the results. The whole atmosphere of their home had changed with the new presentation of each room. It seemed bigger and brighter than before and any buyer would be able to move in without having to worry about having to do more work. The proof of the success was when Billy and Margaret gladly accepted an offer of £4,000 over the asking price!

> **Margaret**
> Every room seems to be more spacious, brighter and lighter

COST	
Paint	£240
Flooring	£150
Bathroom suite	£199
Garden	£135
Accessories	£750
including 'Twiceasquick' wallpaper for bathroom, Colouroll, £10.99 per metre	
Labour	£480
TOTAL	£1,954

AFTER
viewers' comments

'It's a different house – light, airy and clutter free.'

'The whole place looked ten times bigger. You can see there's scope to do something with it.'

'It's not the same house.'

'What can you say ...?'

how to

DRESS WINDOWS

Curtains have many uses – they frame and enhance a window and its view, they help keep the warmth in a room, they act as a shield between you and the world outside and they control the amount of light that enters. Blinds give a clean, uncluttered look on their own but can also work well with curtains to provide privacy or shade. They are particularly useful where curtains are hard to fit, for instance in dormer windows.

curtains

The style of curtain you choose should relate to the style of your room. Take into account the period of your house, the style of your furniture and the existing décor of the room. Take your time in choosing the fabric. Make sure to take sample swatches home so you can test them in the light of the room and against your colour scheme. The ideal curtain length is either to the floor or to the windowsill. Anything in between will not flatter the proportions of the window. You can play with the dimensions of the window by your choice of curtain. A narrow window will look wider if the curtain rail is extended on either side and sill-length curtains are used, while a wide window can be narrowed with floor-length curtains and/or those that cover part of the glass when open.

Curtain accessories

So often in interior design it is the details that count. Curtains must fit, but headings, pelmets and poles should be combined to maximum effect

Headings

Headings are the different kinds of gathers at the top of the curtain, and are often determined by the kind of heading tape used. The most simple is a gathered heading about 2.5cm (1in) deep. Pencil pleats (about 7.5cm/3in deep running continuously across the curtain) and pinch pleats (small groups of pleats occurring at regular intervals) are the most popular. For a more formal effect, you might use box pleats, goblet pleats or lattice pleats. Other types of headings include looped, or tab-top, headings (loops, or tabs, that circle the pole), cased headings (in which two parallel rows of stitching across the top hem create a slot for a curtain pole), wooden, plastic or metal rings sewn directly on to the fabric or simple fabric ties.

Pelmets

Pelmets cover the curtain headings or tracks and can be as simple or as fancy as the mood takes. They are usually made of wood and can be cut into shapes that complement the window. Covered with fabric or just painted, they define the window and can help make a more formal statement.

Tracks and poles

Take as much time to choose your curtain poles or tracks as the curtains themselves. Poles can be plain or decorative and come in a huge range of materials and diameters. Make sure the track or pole is strong enough to bear the weight of your chosen fabric.

Fabric

Never skimp on fabric to save money. Generous curtains look best, so choose cheaper fabric rather than less of it. Large patterns suit big windows and heavy fabrics work best full-length. If you're stuck, try plain cream curtains edged with coordinating fabric.

Tiebacks

These are particularly useful to hold the curtains back out of the way. Whether you want a simple metallic or wooden holdback or a more elaborate fabric tie will depend on the style of your curtains. Tiebacks can be richly tasselled ropes or made of the same fabric as the curtain or pelmet, or made of contrasting fabric.

MEASURING UP

Measuring up correctly is the key to success. To find the correct width, take the following steps:

1 Measure the length of the track, including the overlapping arm if there is one.

2 Decide how full the curtains will be by choosing a heading (see facing page).

3 Multiply the required width by the fullness to get the overall fabric width required.

4 Divide this by the width of the fabric you have chosen to reach the total number of widths required.

5 Measure the length of fabric drop, allowing extra for pattern repeats and hem.

6 Multiply the fabric drop by the number of widths to reach the total length of fabric needed.

blinds

Roller blinds are the simplest type of blind and have the advantage of going with most decorative schemes. You can buy them in easy-to-make kit form. Make sure you choose a tightly woven fabric that will unroll evenly. Alternatively, you can treat a softer material with fabric stiffener. On larger windows, check that the fabric you choose is substantial enough to make the blind hang well. Remember, too, that roller blinds are not usually very successful on a long drop, for instance on a French window.

The choice of fabric can make a big difference to the effect created. For a clean and businesslike look for an office or study, select something plain and smart. For a warmer, homelier look, choose patterns. Plain blinds, especially, look more 'finished' with the addition of an edging. This can be a fringed, braided or scalloped edge, or simply a band of contrasting colour.

Types of blinds

Blinds are the sleek, modern way to dress windows. Available in an array of colours and materials, they are especially useful where space is limited

Roman blinds

Roman blinds are another unfussy solution as versatile as the roller blind. When pulled down, Roman blinds look like their cousins but they pull up in deep folds. Because of this, the 'look' is a bit softer, and many people prefer Roman blinds to the simpler roller blind in living spaces or bedrooms. Unlike roller blinds, Romans are usually lined to make them hang better, with battens sewn into pockets at regular intervals up the back. For the best results you should choose a firmly woven fabric. If you choose a patterned fabric, make sure it is printed squarely on the grain of the fabric.

Austrian blinds

Austrian blinds are the most ornate. They are unlined, often have a scalloped hem and pull up in swags, sometimes with frills at the side or bottom. They may be left at half-mast, and 'soften' a room. This makes them a perfect choice for bedrooms or any room which you want to be cosy. Because they cover quite a lot of window, they are a clever way of disguising an ugly one, or of screening a dull or blank view.

Venetian blinds

Now available in a wide variety of different styles and colours, Venetian blinds don't have to look dull and functional. The ones with narrow slats are immediately much smarter, and the thin-slatted metallic blinds can look wonderful with a hi-tech design – a shining new kitchen for example – or can give a slick, up-to-the-minute look to a study or teenager's room. Finally, don't forget the effect you can get from even the palest sunlight filtering through a lowered Venetian with the slats spread – the pattern on the walls brings you a real feeling of the Mediterranean.

Wooden slats

The 'Earth Mother' alternative to Venetian blinds, wooden slats are usually held by bands of webbing or canvas which come in various colours and textures. Each of these will have a different effect in your room. They go well with stripped floors, natural wood furniture and ethnic fabrics. They are also practical and, when closed, keep in warmth. Louvred shutters are beautiful and serve the same purpose – if you can afford them.

PLANT POTS

Use your imagination to create attractive plant containers
that will brighten up the forgotten areas of your garden

old bucket

What you need

- bucket
- drill
- hammer and nail
- polystyrene pieces
- plastic sheeting
- potting compost
- plants (see below)

1 Take an old bucket and drill some drainage
holes in its base. Alternatively, turn the bucket
upside down and hammer a nail through the
bottom to make several holes.

2 To reduce the depth of the bucket, put in
a layer of polystyrene pieces and cover with
a sheet of plastic pierced with holes.

3 Top up with compost then plant. This
arrangement used pale apricot nicotiana,
verbena, lilac lobelia and helichrysum for
a light summery effect.

USING COMPOST AND FERTILISER

Garden soil can be used in plant containers but it can bring pests, weeds and disease
with it. It is better to use a proprietary brand of potting compost. To encourage growth,
remember to water regularly so that the compost never dries out and use slow-release
fertiliser capsules.

bicycle basket

What you need

- bicycle basket
- hessian, plastic or ready-made liner
- potting compost
- plants (see below)

1 An old bicycle basket can make a great outdoor container for plants. It can be just as easily hung up, stood on a windowsill or attached to a wall through the hole in its back.

2 Line the basket with hessian, a ready-made liner, or plastic with holes punched into it for drainage.

3 Fill with compost then plant. This arrangement used a mix of sky-blue *Convolvulus sabatius*, pale mauve trailing petunia, and a selection of miniature pelargoniums. Together they create a wild, old-fashioned look that tones well with their country setting.

FINDING AND USING OTHER TYPES OF CONTAINER

Look around the house and in junk shops for other items that could be given a new lease of life in your garden. Old, coloured enamel colanders, wire baskets, kettles or butler's sinks are just some of the things that can make plant containers. Add drainage holes where necessary or line with holed plastic so the compost stays in place. Wire baskets look best with an outer lining of moss disguising the plastic lining. Choose plants to complement or contrast with their surroundings.

NEWCASTLE UNDER LYME

Three-bedroom detached house in Westbury Park with small living room leading to kitchen/diner, two double bedrooms, one single bedroom. £76,500.

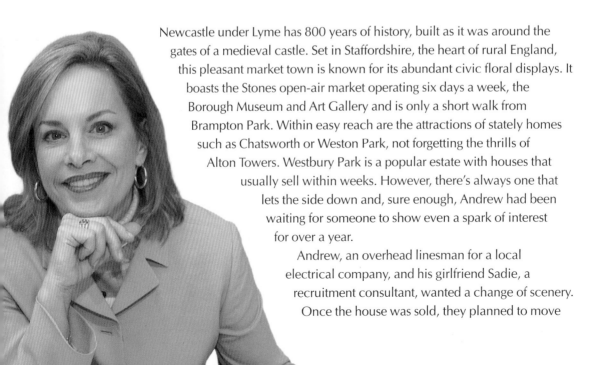

Newcastle under Lyme has 800 years of history, built as it was around the gates of a medieval castle. Set in Staffordshire, the heart of rural England, this pleasant market town is known for its abundant civic floral displays. It boasts the Stones open-air market operating six days a week, the Borough Museum and Art Gallery and is only a short walk from Brampton Park. Within easy reach are the attractions of stately homes such as Chatsworth or Weston Park, not forgetting the thrills of Alton Towers. Westbury Park is a popular estate with houses that usually sell within weeks. However, there's always one that lets the side down and, sure enough, Andrew had been waiting for someone to show even a spark of interest for over a year.

Andrew, an overhead linesman for a local electrical company, and his girlfriend Sadie, a recruitment consultant, wanted a change of scenery. Once the house was sold, they planned to move to Australia. Andrew couldn't see why his home wasn't selling but Sadie put her finger smack on the problems – the décor and the overwhelming and correct impression that it was a bachelor pad.

The welcome to the house was pretty indifferent with a broken doorbell and a vacuum cleaner blocking the way in. But the first thing that hit me was the loud colour scheme. Secondly, it was obvious this was a man's home and as such it didn't have mass appeal. It was so masculine it was off-putting to women buyers so something had to give. I needed to change its look completely so that the property would seem equally attractive to a single woman, a family or a couple.

The saving grace in this project was Sadie – and not just because she turned out to be an ally. She had sold her own home and was storing all her furniture with Andrew's mother so we had a source of new furniture we could have for free. Together we went to war on most of the rooms in this bachelor pad.

Andrew
I'm guilty. I just think of it as a place to eat and sleep. It's a base basically

Doctor's Diagnosis

To make this a spacious family home we had to:

- Lighten and neutralise the living room
- Lay a new floor
- Remove the dog's bed
- Redefine the dining area
- Rearrange and redecorate the master bedroom
- Transform the box room into a spare bedroom

BEFORE
viewers' comments

'My impression is that it hasn't had much love and attention.'

'For me to purchase it, it would need a complete renovation / facelift to alter its appearance dramatically.'

'It needs a lot of work, a lot of decoration and a lot of money spending on it.'

'There's nothing there that makes you feel at home.'

BEFORE

living

It was tough to know where to begin in the living room. When Andrew and his father had installed the wood-burning stove, they had failed to take into account the scale of the furniture. The result was that it looked as if the pieces had been stuffed in. Andrew did have a great colour sense, taking his lead from the pictures in the room, but they were too bold for the size of the room and made it look smaller. I decided everything had to go. The most painful thing for Andrew was the removal of the fireplace he and his father had installed together when he moved in. It may have heated the room effectively but it was too big, making the arrangement of furniture look clumsy and cramped. Removing it meant we could play with the space better.

Before doing that, the hideous Artex ceiling had to be disguised under a coat of Artex that didn't have a dizzying semi-circular finish. Then I turned my attention to

AFTER

the walls, waving goodbye to those bold colours as they disappeared under a layer of undercoat and then a soft neutral. The last thing to contend with was the lino that Andy had never got round to doing anything about. New wood laminate flooring immediately lightened the room and gave it a modern, clean finish. At last it was the turn of the furniture. The hideous leather sofa and chairs had no place in the new scheme of things even though Andrew had only just bought them, having wanted such a suite for as long as he could remember. But I wanted something less intrusively masculine. This is where Sadie's stash of possessions came into use. Her blue and white sofa and chair were the perfect answer. Without being too feminine, they were softer and made the room look more lived in. They also established a new colour scheme, matching with the wallpaper in the kitchen. Andrew loved his sound systems but agreed he couldn't listen to two at once. He packed one away so that the other and the TV could be neatly tucked away under the stairs, with CDs racked on the wall.

The living room was divided from the kitchen by a dimpled glass partition and solid door. More light was let into the room by putting glass panels in the door. To make the kitchen less obvious behind the glass, I hung some sheer fabric in front of it. This still let the light through but created a wonderful unexpected watery effect as well. This room really lived up to the maxim, 'less is more'. By toning everything down and introducing a more feminine touch, the room now looked as if it might be part of a family home.

kitchen/dining

The kitchen itself needed very little attention, because the colour scheme worked well with Sadie's furniture. Andrew had done a good job of remodelling it but had left the boiler exposed in all its glory. It was quite simple to have a joiner box it in using MDF. As there weren't any upper units, I felt the kitchen looked better balanced with the addition of a couple of white shelves for storage. However, the room as a whole needed bringing together so that it looked more up to date and operated better as one. To begin with, I continued the new flooring used in the living room through into the kitchen. This had the overall effect of making the whole ground floor flow together but also making

AFTER

it look both smarter and more contemporary. Wood laminate is an ideal finish for a kitchen floor, being hard-wearing and easy to keep clean.

Looking at the dining end of the room, one thing was obvious. Andrew's boxer, George, and his bed would have to be found a new home in the garage outside. Apart from the fact that some buyers might be unnerved by the presence of a dog, many would be put off by its smell and by the fact that it was unhygienic having him in the kitchen. The heavy dresser wasn't doing the space any favours, but then neither did the large radiator that lurked behind it. The problem was solved with a wide radiator cover that could double as a sideboard. The wall space above was ideal for display shelves. The walls were lifted with a coat of soft sunshine yellow paint. We bought a round table for the centre of the room with some foldaway chairs, and the room presented the image of a lifestyle anyone would happily aspire to.

AFTER

master bedroom

The master bedroom was small and needed to be given an added sense of space to justify its definition as the principal sleeping space. This was achieved quite simply by painting the room a soothing pale green and by moving the bed to become the focal point. The dark blue accents of the lightshade, new checked bedlinen and the deep green cushions made a dramatic contrast against the walls.

AFTER

box room

Andrew was wasting the box room. Stuffed with a bed that Andrew had yet to finish making, the laundry and the ironing board, it looked more like an enormous cupboard. It is essential to make every room work towards getting that sale. So we finished it by tidying away the clutter, which was helped by boxing in the space under the bed to create a storage area. It was now on its way to becoming a single room. Fixing the doors to the cupboard under the bed gave the room a cleaner finish. Then the walls were painted a discreet blush pink. All that was needed was a new duvet to give it a bit of class plus some Chinese symbols on the wall, inspired by the new bedding.

At last Andrew and Sadie were looking at a home with a friendly, fashionable feel, light years away from its previous look. Would it be enough to enable them to realise their dream of taking off for Australia? Sure enough, within a month they had accepted an offer of the asking price, and Sadie had accepted the offer of Andrew's hand in marriage. A satisfactory outcome all round.

```
COST
Paint                        £100
   including 'Chelsea Green',
   Crown Paints, £13.99
   per 2.5 litres
Laminate flooring            £180
Carpet                        £75
Accessories                  £369
   including '1103' radiator
   cover, Jali, £169
   'Zen' embellished
   single duvet set,
   Take Cover, £28
Labour                       £500

TOTAL                      £1,224
```

'**Sadie**
I like the living room and the box room in particular. They're fabulous'

AFTER
viewers' comments

'It's so different, you wouldn't believe it was the same house.'

'I would say it was worth the asking price and worth considering quite seriously.'

'A lot brighter and a lot more space.'

'I like the floor. It sets everything off.'

how to

REVAMP SOFAS AND CHAIRS

Tired old sofas and armchairs that look as if they've lost their bounce can be brought back to life fairly simply and inexpensively

cushions

If it's just a question of your sofa looking neglected, have it professionally cleaned and add some contrasting cushions.

Cushions come in limitless sizes and shapes and are useful for introducing colour, texture and a feeling of comfort. They can coordinate or contrast with the other surfaces and colours in a room and can be used to inject a bit of zip into a depressed piece of furniture.

cover-up job

If a more drastic cover-up is needed, the easiest thing is to cover either a sofa or an armchair with a throw. There is a large range of designs and colours available to transform not only the furniture but the whole look of a room. If you don't want to go to the expense of buying a throw, good alternatives are bedspreads, rugs, antique and modern shawls. All of these have the advantage of protecting the sofa from further damage, disguising the damage that has already been done and introducing colour and texture into a room. A disadvantage is the way they will slip untidily out of place unless firmly secured.

A throw can be simply draped over the piece of furniture and held in place by cushions. Greater security is achieved by tucking it into the sides and back of the sofa.

To make sure your throw is big enough to do this, measure the sofa from front to back adding at least another 30cm (12in) to accommodate the tuck, and from side to side adding another 60cm (24in). Don't skimp. Alternatively, use one throw for the back of the sofa, another for the seat and others over the arms. Small, specialist spiral pins are sold to hold throws in place.

loose covers

A more expensive solution is to make or buy loose covers. They will give your sofa or chair a new look at less cost than buying a new one. Stick to medium-weight fabrics and, if the covers are washable, check they are shrinkproof. To look their best they need to be carefully measured and fitted, although if you are lucky you may find the perfect off-the-peg solution.

Dining-room chairs can also be given a new lease of life. If they are wooden, they can be touched up with woodstain and varnish, or painted. Add colour and comfort by adding cushions, perhaps even with ties to fasten to the chairback and legs. If the seat is removable, a new cover is the answer. It is a simple matter to remove the seat, lay it upside down on a new piece of fabric, then pull the fabric taut over the top and tack or staple it in place underneath, carefully pleating the corners before neatening the base by covering it with a piece of plain tough fabric.

A more dramatic solution is a simple slip-over cover that reaches to just below the seat or to the floor. Made up from a pattern of squares and rectangles, a simple slipcover may have inverted pleats over each leg, button-up backs or tied sides or back.

When choosing new fabric, remember what else is in the room when you look at different textures, colours and patterns. If you are unsure in your choice, it is often wise to go for a neutral colour, relying on its texture for interest. Then, when it is in situ, dress it up with a coloured cushion or two that will tie it in with the general colour scheme.

RESTYLED TABLE AND CHAIRS

Give an uninspiring set of table and chairs some pizzazz
with a lick of paint, colourful fabric and a glass table top

What you need

- table and chairs
  with removable
  seats
- protective face
  mask
- medium-grade
  sandpaper
- paintbrush, small
  emulsion roller
  and tray
- water-based
  primer
- emulsion paint
- ruler and tape
  measure
- stencil acetate
- Chinagraph pencil
- craft knife and
- cutting mat
- stencil brush
- clear acrylic
  varnish
- scissors
- fabric
- spray adhesive
- safety glass with
  bevelled edges for
  table top
- pliers and
  screwdriver
- thin upholstery
  foam for chair
  seats
- fabric marker pen
- staple gun

1 Remove the seats from the chairs and,
wearing a face mask for protection, sand all
the wooden surfaces. Wipe clean and paint
on water-based primer. When dry, paint the
table and the chairs with two coats of
emulsion, allowing the first coat to dry
before applying the second.

2 Measure the table top and work out the size of a square that will divide into both the table's length and width. Make a stencil by drawing parallel lines on the acetate with a Chinagraph pencil. Mark into squares and cut out alternate ones using a craft knife.

3 Stencil a row of squares all around the table an equal distance apart. Stencil a second row inside them to create a chessboard effect. When the paint is dry, apply two coats of varnish to both the table and the chairs, again allowing the first coat to dry before applying the second.

4 Measure the area of the table inside the chequered border and cut a piece of fabric to fit. For a neater edge, allow a 1cm (⅜in) hem. Press the fabric then spray the wrong side with adhesive before laying it carefully on the centre of the table. Place the glass on top.

5 Remove the old fabric and any staples or nails from the chair seats. Draw the outline of a chair seat and add 2cm (¾in) all round. Cut new pieces of foam to this size. Spray the seats with adhesive and stick the foam in place.

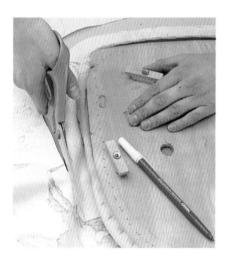

6 Lay the new fabric for each chair seat, right side facing down, on a flat surface. Put the seat on top and draw around it, allowing an extra 5cm (2in) all the way round. Cut out the fabric.

7 Fold in the edges of the fabric and staple to the underside of each seat. Staple first one then the opposite edge of the seat, alternating so that the fabric can be pulled to fit tightly across. Pleat the fabric carefully at the corners. Replace the seats in the chairs.

Use different fabric in the same way to create
an entirely different effect. Pretty floral patterns
will be at home in the country, while bright
geometrics will suit a contemporary room. Plain
coloured tops will claim less attention if there
are other patterns working elsewhere in the
room but will help create a coordinated look.

GARELOCHHEAD

Splendid four-bedroom detached Victorian villa overlooking Gareloch, with two reception rooms, large kitchen, study, two bathrooms, substantial garden. Great views. Offers over £145,000.

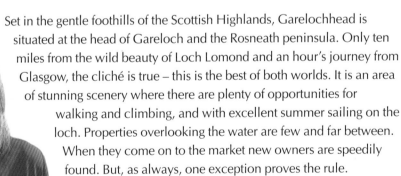

Set in the gentle foothills of the Scottish Highlands, Garelochhead is situated at the head of Gareloch and the Rosneath peninsula. Only ten miles from the wild beauty of Loch Lomond and an hour's journey from Glasgow, the cliché is true – this is the best of both worlds. It is an area of stunning scenery where there are plenty of opportunities for walking and climbing, and with excellent summer sailing on the loch. Properties overlooking the water are few and far between. When they come on to the market new owners are speedily found. But, as always, one exception proves the rule.

Glaswegian Kenny, his Polish wife Angie and their eleven-year-old son, Leo, lived in an imposing Victorian mansion with superb views across the loch below. They were reluctant to leave but the house had become too much for them to run so they had bought a plot of land and were planning on building a smaller house to their specifications. They had absolutely no idea why their current house wasn't selling and, by the time we met, they were willing to do anything that would help shift it.

The house itself was magnificent, standing alone in its rural setting. But I was stopped in my tracks as I crossed the threshold. I had never seen a Polish/Scottish Victorian house before. Angie had made her distinctive mark, even in the hallway. I could see immediately that she liked bright colours (pink and red) and that she was a collector. The rooms were typically Victorian, large with high ceilings, but it was difficult to get a clear impression of their dimensions thanks to the plethora of possessions. Would Kenny and Angie agree to packing away at least half of them?

Having looked around the whole house, I decided that the best thing to do was focus on the ground floor. Time didn't allow us to cover the whole house and if we could get the buyers to love the main floor, I hoped they would be sold on the place by the time they got upstairs. This was a wonderful house with many original features that hadn't been brought out to their full potential. I decided to focus on them by cutting back on the clutter and redecorating.

Doctor's Diagnosis
To restore grandeur to the house we had to:
• Tame the décor
• Clear the clutter
• Focus on the original features

BEFORE
viewers' comments

'My husband tells me to look past the décor but I couldn't. There's far too much junk in there.'

'It's got a lot of potential. But for that asking price? I wouldn't pay that.'

'I certainly wouldn't put in an offer unless it was gutted inside.'

'Dull, dark and dreary.'

Angie
I thought my house was nice

BEFORE

entrance

The first striking thing about the hall was its lack of period feel and the second was the colours that brought the walls inwards, minimising the space. Once I'd got rid of the horses adorning the wall and the intrusive side table, we could get to work on my mission to reinstate the house's former glory. I nervously ordered the flat modern façades to be removed from the doors. Sure enough, behind them were the original panelled doors in good enough condition to need only a little restoration. Once they'd been sanded down, filled, had some beading added and been painted, they looked as good as new. Then it was the turn of the walls.

The vinyl wallpaper and pattern borders were stripped off to make way for some stick-on, paintable wood-panelling. This was extremely easy to fit, needing tacking only where we felt it needed the extra hold. Once

AFTER

the dado rail had been fitted and the walls and woodwork painted, the hall was beginning to take shape. The modern radiator, one of my pet hates, was an anachronism but a necessity so the best we could do was box it in. I wanted to add a little warmth by picking up the red from the runner and hanging a curtain in the same shade at the end of the corridor. The final key to the transformation was replacing the green carpet with one in a cool neutral shade. Now there was an entrance in keeping with the fine exterior of the house.

BEFORE

dining

The dining room had been taken over by Kenny as a music room. His keyboard stood waiting to be played in front of a photographic audience of friends and family. Although there was a substantial dining table, a computer had also found a place in the room so anyone entering wouldn't know why they were there. Was this a dining room, music room or office? It is important to make it plain to buyers what they are looking at, so they can imagine how to use the room themselves. This dining room was too good to be anything else so Kenny had to find another home for his instruments, at least three-quarters of his audience and the computer. Family photos should not be on display apart from in the more personal parts of the house, otherwise

AFTER

the buyer becomes distracted from the matter in hand. As with the hall, I brought out the period features – in this case by removing the mountains of clutter so they could be seen more clearly. Shelves were tidied, pictures were thinned out and the furniture polished till it gleamed. The chandelier was 'antiqued' with a good spray of metallic paint. (Remember, this treatment should only be done out of doors.) Another touch was the addition of period light switches and door handles. It's always worth paying attention to such details. Before moving the furniture back in, a new light-coloured carpet was added to lift the room. The best moment of all was saying goodbye to those over-ornate curtains and replacing them with cool louvre shutters. The dining table and chairs were extremely handsome and were complemented by one or two other pieces such as the window seat and corner cupboard. When we'd finished, we had a dining room fit for a king.

AFTER

living

As far as accumulating things went, this room was the worst. Angie had made it a particularly personal space full of pictures and ornaments and naturally her favourite colours. Of course, there is absolutely nothing wrong with dressing a room to your own taste. It only becomes a problem when you are trying to sell the house and buyers' attentions are caught by what's in the room and not by the room itself.

I knew there was another room inside this one dying to get out. The only way to find it was to bring in professional packers who were able to put most of Angie's treasures into storage until such time as they were needed again. One of the key features in the room was the bay window with a view. I felt this could be played up significantly and was delighted to find that Angie had taken out a previous window seat. When we found the pieces, they were too warped to be used again but they were good enough to use as a pattern for cutting MDF to size. The old cushions were dug out and reupholstered to fit properly. Then I set Angie to the sewing machine where she ran up the curtains to frame the window. The other feature that was almost completely hidden was the grand fireplace. Its pre-eminence was restored and the gloomy picture above it was replaced by a mirror to provide a much clearer focal point. The striped wallpaper was primed so that the stripes wouldn't show through the subtle new wall colour and the removal of the rug contributed to the new sense of serenity I was aiming for. In the end we had an elegant, period room that was completely in keeping with the rest of the house.

dressing

As dressing rooms go, this was a nightmare. When I first went in, I was stunned. A study had been given over to Angie's extensive wardrobe and had become her dressing room. I couldn't believe the amount of clothes she owned. Suddenly, the arena of war had changed and I could see that this was where I was going to have most trouble. Angie painfully went through all her clothes, sorting out which ones she wanted to keep or to store and which could go to charity. I was determined to transform this huge walk-in wardrobe into a neat little study. Once its contents were removed, we could get at the huge wall map to 'antique' it with a spirit and woodstain mixture. Then it was simply a question of dressing the room with a few pieces of furniture in the room in order to give it an identity. I was

able to work with what Kenny and Angie already had, which meant that the red accents throughout the house could be echoed in here with the chairs. This was the smallest room but it saw the biggest change and undoubtedly added to the value of the house.

kitchen

Lastly, we attended to the kitchen. Despite my initial trepidation it turned out to be better than I was expecting. All it required was some rejigging and cleaning. The only major changes I made were to eliminate the carpet tiles in favour of practical vinyl

flooring and to add some appropriate wallpaper behind the trelliswork. After that it was simply a staging story, removing much of Angie's wall decorations and anything that obstructed the view, changing the table for a wooden-topped one that fitted in with the rural theme, and adding a few pots of herbs, a bowl of fruit and various select pieces of china.

I was delighted when the work was finished. I felt this faded lady of a house had had her original character revived and now presented a much more stylish and desirable face to the world. And sure enough, it was only a matter of weeks before Kenny and Angie were considering two offers from buyers who had responded to her seductive charms.

By June the house had been sold for more than the asking price.

```
COST
Paint                      £205
Flooring                   £492
  including carpet,
  Carpet Right, £5.97
  per square metre
Hall panelling             £225
  EASIPanel
Accessories              £1,196
  including louvre
  shutters, The Shutter
  Shop, £700
  light switches,
  Classy Brass, £12.99
  door handles,
  Clayton Monroe,
  £41 per pair
  radiator cover,
  Jali, £195
Labour                     £650

TOTAL                    £2,768
```

Kenny
It's a good house in a good situation and Ann has gift-wrapped it

AFTER
viewers' comments

'It was as though we'd walked into a new house. Lovely.'

'The whole place is uncluttered so you can see four walls in each room.'

'I think the interior now matches the exterior.'

how to

DISPLAY ITEMS

Displaying collections such as china, silver, tins or ornaments needs to be thought through carefully. Having too many pieces crammed into a space does neither the space nor the objects justice. All it shows is the impressive size of the collection and the fact that you don't have room to accommodate it. If necessary, rotate the collection so that it can be truly appreciated. A large collection can be displayed in different rooms.

pictures

If hung well, pictures lend character and warmth to a room. Single pictures may be hung symmetrically, possibly balancing a mirror or a piece of furniture. If you don't want a regimented sense of order then create a more asymmetrical look by visually balancing a large picture against a number of smaller ones, remembering that each side of the composition should take up the same square footage. When using pictures to create an impact, bear in mind that a strong unifying look can be achieved by using the same frames and mounts. If they are unevenly sized, the composition needs to be worked out before hanging the pictures on the wall. Measure the wall space you want them to occupy then lay the pictures on the floor to occupy the right shape, working out the right balance. If unsure, make paper silhouettes and tape them to the wall first to see the effect.

books

Books furnish a room but not if they are stuffed randomly into shelves or left higgledy-piggledy on tables or the floor. They can give colour, texture and definition to a room if they are given proper space.

When planning to house your books, think of the shelving as a design feature not just a necessity. The inside of a bookcase might be painted a different colour to that of the walls or wood might be stained to match the furniture in the room. Objects displayed beside your books will offset their shape and create a sense of depth and space in the room.

Bookshelves can bring elements in a room together. They can frame doors or windows, unifying the spaces between them. They can also act as a focal point, for example cubed shelves arranged in a geometric pattern against a wall become a feature. They can also frame a focal point if they are built into alcoves on either side of a chimneybreast, bed or window seat. If buying furniture, think about how it might be used for books, for example a small bookcase can double as an occasional table by a sofa. A sofa in the middle of a room might back on to a low bookcase rather than a table. The space beneath a window seat or bed could be converted into bookshelves. A wide passage between rooms or a stairway might be transformed by the addition of floor-to-ceiling bookcases. Remember, this sort of library needs to be well lit so that it doesn't seem poky and so that the contents of the library can be seen. Wherever the shelves, do not overcrowd them. Take time to weed out the books you're unlikely to read again and give them to charity.

REVAMPED FOOTSTOOL

Some simple upholstery techniques are enough to give
a new lease of life to a tired old stool

What you need

- old stool
- screwdriver
- varnish remover
- fine-grade sandpaper
- antique brown wax
  and soft cloth

- serrated knife
- 10cm (4in) thick foam
- PVA glue
- scissors
- lining fabric
- staple gun

- upholstery fabric
- tape measure
- decorative trim
- hammer and
  upholstery studs

1 Carefully remove the studs, staples, tacks and seat pad from your old footstool. Use varnish remover on the wood and then clean it with soapy water. When dry, lightly sand and rub wax into the wood. Give it a gentle sheen by buffing with a soft cloth.

2 Using a serrated knife, cut thick foam to fit the stool top. Cut out wedges to give rounded corners so that the material will cover without creasing. Cover the stool top with PVA glue. Press the foam down hard and leave until stuck firmly in place.

3 Cut lining fabric to fit the foam. Staple the fabric to the stool on one side before pulling it tightly across and fixing it on the opposite side. Pleat the fabric to avoid rucking as you staple. Cut off the excess. Cover the stool with upholstery fabric using the same technique.

4 Measure the decorative trim so that it runs all round the stool. Use it to cover the raw fabric edges, sticking it in place with PVA glue. To make sure it stays in place, hammer in studs at regular intervals.

BRISTOL

Four-bedroom, single-storey house with one reception room, large kitchen/dining area leading to walled patio, study, bathroom, separate toilet, large garden. £299,950.

Bristol is the largest city in southwest England, set in the midst of rolling countryside not far from the seaside resort of Weston-Super-Mare. Bristol was home to the Victorian engineer Isambard Kingdom Brunel, who designed the Clifton suspension bridge, and was once famous for its busy trading port from which John Cabot embarked on his voyage to discover Newfoundland. A fine historic city, it has many notable houses, heritage estates, churches and chapels to be visited, supported by various galleries and museums. In the summer the city comes to life with such highlights as the regatta, the St Paul's Carnival and kite and hot air balloon festivals. There are also a number of first-rate theatres, cinemas and concert halls. Bristol is a popular university city, with a thriving street scene and vibrant nightlife. With two train stations, it is easily accessible from most parts of the UK. Despite some war damage to the centre of the city, there is still a plethora of stunning Victorian and Georgian buildings and, as in most cosmopolitan cities, the property market is always humming. That is particularly true in leafy suburbs such as Cotham, only five minutes from the city centre.

But there's always one that doesn't sell. This time it was a secluded bungalow called Butterfly Cottage. It had been on the market for four months without so much as an offer. Hidden away behind walls smothered in climbing plants, it was in an idyllic spot, as peaceful as being in the depths of the country. It belonged to Lesley, who moved there in 1992 having fallen in love with it at first sight. She was leaving reluctantly because she was mid-divorce and having to sell up so she and her son Jamie could move elsewhere. Having reacted so positively when she first saw the property herself almost ten years earlier, she was mystified as to why it hadn't sold immediately.

I didn't find it so hard to see why. For a start I had trouble finding it, the walls and nameplate were so overgrown, and I wasn't too keen on the 'Beware the Dog' notice. Although tiny details, they might be enough to make a buyer approach the property in a slightly negative frame of mind. Why risk it when they are easy to fix? Lesley showed me around the side of the house so that we entered straight through French windows into the living room, avoiding the front door altogether. It may have been more convenient, but it went against the design and flow of the house. Much better to come in through the front door and follow the house's natural progression, ending in the wonderful living room overlooking the garden. Showing it backwards would confuse buyers. The house itself was delightful, the setting and location were unbeatable. However, I felt that it was a bit 'shabby chic' with some fabulous antiques rubbing shoulders with too much tatty furniture. It felt homely but tired and was crying out for a facelift. So we set to work.

Doctor's Diagnosis

To give the house life we had to:
- Re-establish the front entrance
- Concentrate on the kitchen and bathroom
- Declutter
- Redecorate

BEFORE
viewers' comments

'For the money, it's terrible.'

'There's a completely confusing issue of colours in this house.'

'You expect at least a decent kitchen.'

'If it was me, I'd gut the place.'

AFTER

entrance

Because Lesley rarely used the front door as an entrance, the hallway had been sadly neglected and was just a long, dark passageway. It really was the weakest link in the place. As I was reinstating the front door to its proper use, it was essential to make the hall somewhere welcoming that would draw the interested buyer into the rest of the house. One of its main features was an ugly radiator, which I immediately had boxed in. Then we wired in some discreet uplighters, which transformed the dreary space into something more glamorous and bright. The lino at the entrance was worn and certainly didn't spell out luxury, so this provided the ideal opportunity to replace it with new laminate wood-effect flooring, which looked much more tasteful and fitted in with the cottagey feel of the property. Fortunately, there was nothing wrong with the carpet that a professional clean wouldn't cure. The walls were painted a warm neutral with white woodwork. Once the doors and frames were in matching white, they helped to unify and magnify the space. A mirror and a few carefully hung pictures made the extra difference. The mirror reflected additional light into the space while the pictures were spaced so they didn't oppose one another and gave an illusion of extra width. I made a feature of the radiator cover by placing the mirror above it and arranging a couple of candles and a plant as welcoming touches.

Lesley
It's a bit like living in the Ideal Home Exhibition where I can't move anything. But it's only for a short period of time

Jamie's room

Children's rooms often let the side down and Jamie's was no exception. Although he kept everything in order, the room was over-crowded and had some particularly unattractive spray paintings on the wall. Lesley left it to me to crack the whip and Jamie was soon grudgingly thinning out his possessions and priming over his decorations so they wouldn't show under the new paint colour I was planning. He was extremely unhappy that his shelving was being reduced so drastically. It was generally too tatty or damaged to belong in his new-look room but we reached a compromise with me agreeing to let him have a few shelves back. The walls looked better in a restful pale green, contrasting with the deep blue carpet and curtains. A work area was created in the alcove with a desk and three shelves. All the surfaces were cleared and clothes put away so the room and its potential could be seen clearly.

BEFORE

AFTER

BEFORE

master bedroom

The master bedroom needed very little doing to it. It was very pretty and private with a great view into the garden. The bed was very awkwardly positioned, 'like a daybed gone wrong', so we turned it to face into the room. This left space for the rest of the furniture to be repositioned in a way that made the room look bigger. The dressing table looked better in front of the window where it was framed by some very pretty new curtains in sheer fabric. All that remained was to work with what was already there, rehanging pictures more carefully and adding a useful small shelf unit. Lastly, we made the bed with new bedlinen and added a couple of toning cushions. Those few touches were enough to change a friendly but untidy bedroom into a tranquil sanctuary that no one could resist.

AFTER

bathroom

It seemed odd to me to have a separate toilet next door to the shower room. It didn't take much to make both of them look fantastic so that no one would immediately think they had to rip them out and start again. The budget didn't run to new units, so I decided to make cosmetic changes by painting and changing the flooring in order to unify the rooms. I worked around the pink, introducing a toning colour on the walls. I linked the rooms together by using the same paint and by introducing identical vinyl flooring in both. Replacing the picture in the toilet with a mirror helped make the room look bigger. Once the two rooms complemented one another, they needed only a few accessories to complete the picture. Fluffy new towels and decorative objects arranged sparely on shelves were enough.

AFTER

BEFORE

kitchen/dining

New kitchens are expensive and this one was quietly asking to be replaced. It is a terrible mistake to let buyers get a whiff of the idea that they may have to invest in a new kitchen. If they do, they will either look for another property or try to negotiate the price down. It's vital to present your kitchen looking its absolute best. Lesley had knocked two rooms into one to create a large, light kitchen and dining room. At the kitchen end, there were brown cupboards and white cupboards and tiles that had

AFTER

Lesley
It's made me look at my house in a different way

obviously been painted over. To achieve a uniform look, we painted the cupboards white and added new handles. Then the tiles were scrubbed and regrouted and given a new lease of life with the addition of suitable ceramic appliqués. The walls were painted a light summery green. We gave the floor a country look by laying a slab-patterned Texline floorcovering. The view through the window was framed by draping a rustic fabric around it to match the new curtains at the French doors. All that remained was to give the whole place a bit of elbow grease and clear the worktops. Lesley wasn't convinced that a kitchen could function without a toaster and kettle on display. I succeeded in persuading her that if she wanted to sell her house, it could. Without too much effort, that end of the room had been made to look much smarter and yet its essence remained unchanged. The dining end of the room looked like a bit of an afterthought. It didn't feel terribly inviting although the change of wall colour and floorcovering made a difference and began to tie the two ends of the room together. A mirror on the far wall reflected the kitchen, and the country dresser was improved once its contents were thinned out and rearranged. Having neutralised the room, I used the curtains to bring in colour and frame the patio. Lastly, some bright flowers and a new lightshade finished it off.

living

The living room was characterised by an eclectic mix of elegant and shabby. It had a country, homely feel but didn't have quite enough style to make up the buyer's mind in favour of the house. Now the front door was re-established, this was the room where the buyer would finish his tour and I wanted to make it the jewel in the crown. In fact I didn't have to do a lot. We changed the paint colours and got rid of the dated orange. Then it was a question of thinning out the furniture and clutter, removing the throws that looked as if they were disguising something much worse than they were. I took the rug away so nothing spoilt the simple elegance established in the room.

AFTER

When our work was finished, I felt the house had been raised to the same standard throughout so that as buyers took their final step into the living room, they'd be sold. The last I heard was that there had been a lot of renewed interest in the house and Lesley and Jamie were hoping for an offer soon.

```
COST
Paint                        £347
Flooring                     £442
Patio, including
water feature                £186
Accessories                £1,162
  including 'San Marco' tile
  appliqués, SM Ceramics, £4 each
  Victorian knobs,
  Knobs and Knockers, £1.60 each
  radiator cover,
  Winther Brown, £16
  shelf kit,
  Focus Do It All, £2.45
Labour                       £417

TOTAL                      £2,454
```

AFTER
viewers' comments

'Amazing what a paint job can do.'

'Homely, warm and a lot smarter.'

'Much more modern looking.'

'The hallway is so much better and more inviting.'

how to

CREATE A FOCAL POINT

Every room needs a focal point. It is the element that grounds the space and focuses your attention on entering. It gives the room a centre, and brings disparate elements together. Display it well, arranging furniture and artefacts around it. It is possible to have more than one focal point in a room as long as one is subordinate. A fireplace may be highlighted in the winter, while a plant or picture window may be the summer's focus.

fireplaces

If your room does have a beautiful fireplace, make the most of it. Remove any clutter that may be obscuring it, clean it thoroughly and polish any fire irons or surround. Focus attention on it by clearing the mantelpiece of accumulated photographs, invitations and general detritus, and arranging only one or two objects in their place. Hang a large mirror or picture above so that the eye is not distracted by too many different elements. A fire always gives the subliminal message that the living room is the heart of the home but if you are unable to light one, burning candles in the grate can be equally attractive. Arrange the furniture around it, so that it becomes the unmistakable centrepiece of the room.

Alternative focal points

Stretch your imagination beyond the obvious. There are many different potential focal points beyond windows and fireplaces

Furniture

If your room is not blessed with either a fireplace or a view worth highlighting, look at the largest pieces of furniture in the room. A dining-room table, an armoire, dresser or a bed could all be the focal point of a room. The key is to ensure that the piece is positioned correctly. If the room is symmetrical the focal point should be placed centrally. Tables should be beautifully laid or have a central decoration or runner. Beds should be made with clean linen with scatter cushions accentuating the colour scheme in the room, while cupboard doors should be firmly shut with nothing hanging from them and dressers should be used to display only a select number of objects.

Artwork

Sometimes a focal point can be created using striking artwork. This may either take the form of a single picture or of a carefully arranged group (see How to display items, on page 58). It may work well for one wall to be painted a different colour, placing the focus on to a wall sculpture, display shelves or a picture. Lighting can play a key part in enhancing the focal point.

The decoration applied to a room can best help the focal point by not being too busy. Too many clashing patterns and colours will compete with it and prevent it from being the star of the show.

feature windows

Another focal point might be a stunning view through a window. Emphasise it by dressing the window appropriately. It might be enough just to paint the window frame a contrasting colour. Otherwise there are all sorts of blinds, curtains and drapes that could be used (see How to dress windows, page 32). When dressing the window take into account its size and the style of the rest of the room. Swags and tails will not look good in a minimalist environment or on a modest casement window. Other ways of drawing attention to the window might include the addition of a built-in bay window seat, window boxes on the outside ledge, a single table in front of it or an ornament on the ledge. Again, it is important to orientate the furniture so that the view isn't blocked by anything too large and can be seen from all vantage points in the room.

GILDED MIRROR FRAME

Mix metallic gold leaf and a bold coloured paint to
give a fabulous finish to an old frame

What you need

- old wooden frame
- medium-grade
  sandpaper
- small paintbrushes
- deep red acrylic
  stencil paint
- gold size (from art
  shop)

- talcum powder
- Dutch metal leaf
  (from art shop)
- scissors and ruler
- wrapping paper
- mirror glass
  (cut to fit)

1 Sand the frame and wipe it clean. Paint
it with acrylic stencil paint, brushing along
the grain of the wood. Leave to dry.

2 Working over a small area at a time,
brush gold size over the edges of the frame,
omitting the central recess. Leave for about
ten minutes to allow the size to become
tacky. Dust your fingers with talcum powder
so the gold leaf will not stick to them.

3 Place a sheet of gold leaf, silver side down, on the size. Smooth it on then peel off the backing paper. Brush size on to the next section and smooth on more gold leaf, just overlapping it with the last. The patchy effect gives an aged look.

4 Cut four strips of wrapping paper to fit the frame's recess. Be sure to mitre the corners precisely so that they match exactly.

5 Brush gold size along the recess and stick the strips of wrapping paper in place, carefully lining up the mitred corners. Hide the joins by covering them with a motif cut out from the wrapping paper. Mount the mirror glass in the frame.

HOVE

Luxury flat with light
and airy hall, open-plan
living/dining room,
small but functional
kitchen with balcony,
large master bedroom
with en suite bathroom,
second bedroom, guest
bedroom, shower room.
Sea views. £250,000.

Hove is a sophisticated resort on the sunny (!) south coast of England,
only a stone's throw from Brighton. It's a popular resort, which buzzes
with life thanks to its many bars, restaurants and clubs. Known as
'Notting Hill on Sea', it is only an hour's train ride from London so it is
popular with commuters. As a result, the property market there is alive
and well with prices ranging from £1,000,000 for a four-bedroom
regency house to £50,000 for a studio flat and £850 for an enviable
beach hut! And nothing stays on the market for long.

Nothing, that is, apart from the home of Richard and
his Brazilian wife, Erica. It had been languishing on the market
for an unbelievable two years. Richard was an auctioneer and
fine art dealer who sold paintings on cruise liners while Erica
worked as a hostess on the Newhaven–Dieppe ferry. They
were planning on exchanging the English sunshine of Hove
for the sunshine of Florida – and who could blame them? –
so the failure to sell

their house was frustrating, especially for Richard who was used to selling things fast. The only negative thing Erica could put her finger on was the colours in the kitchen. Their estate agent was also mystified by the lack of success. Situated in a sought-after street, with sea views, an apartment like this should sell immediately. In despair they asked for my help.

My first impressions were generally favourable. It was a large airy apartment with great views but it had a just-moved-in feel to it. The walls were too bare, not all the windows had curtains and the objects picked up on their travels all competed with one another. Even after a quick tour, I could immediately see what could be done to maximise its selling potential. It was being advertised as a 'luxury' flat and it was the 'luxury' that was missing here. I usually advise clients to neutralise and depersonalise their homes but here they couldn't have gone more neutral. This was a case of having to inject some style with colour and by thinning out and rearranging possessions. This property went on the market in the 20th century so I planned to bring it kicking and screaming into the 21st. I knew my reaction depressed Richard, but if I wasn't honest I'd be wasting their time.

Doctor's Diagnosis

To give it the luxury prospective buyers will expect we had to:
- Tidy up
- Thin out the knick knacks
- Divide the living/dining areas
- Turn the storage room into a bedroom
- Modernise the kitchen
- Introduce new colour schemes

BEFORE
viewers' comments

'For that price, I think it could be much better.'

'It's not "luxury", is it?'

'Not the wonderful master bedroom I'd have expected. It's the magnolia syndrome.'

'To consider putting in an offer, we'd have to see a new kitchen.'

AFTER

entrance

The entrance hall gave a nice welcome but the bare magnolia walls were particularly unfriendly and the big piece of furniture with the Buddha on it was a bit heavy on the eye. A simple solution was to hang a few well-placed pictures and use one particularly fine set of shelves as a focal point.

BEFORE

living/dining

This was a lovely, big airy room but there was too much going on in it. Different styles and objects were vying with one another for attention. The formal table and chairs from Richard's mother's house and the cosy sofa and chair rubbed up uneasily against the oriental treasures brought back from their travels. There were too many things detracting from the feeling of space, making it hard to appreciate fully either the room or its wonderful contents. The elegant fireplace was almost completely hidden behind a small statue. And where were the curtains? It's true the flat was too high up to invite the stares of neighbours or passers-by but a view should be framed if it is to be appreciated at its best. As for the floor – I immediately spotted a stain that Erica had tried to sand away but had only made worse and then abandoned. DIY jobs must be completed

AFTER

before putting a home on the market – all they do is draw the eye away from the good points of a room.

The first thing I wanted to do here was cover the damage on the floor with a special felt-tip pen containing woodstain and spirit. Obviously it can't be used on a whole floor but it was perfect for disguising a small area of botched DIY.

Then we went through Richard and Erica's belongings, weeding them out, rehanging pictures and arranging a few key pieces so each one could be highlighted and individually enjoyed. Despite the undoubted quality of their foreign treasures, there was no need to have them all on display at once. I restored the fireplace as the focal point of the room by removing the statue that was blocking it.

It was such a large space that I felt we could afford to distinguish the living and dining areas. I find screens are often very effective because they give a sense of division without blocking the light or breaking up the space too much. In this case, I wanted to give the room a bit of added pizzazz so I designed a screen based on the nearby Brighton Pavilion.

Serendipitously, it had romantic connotations for Richard and Erica who had got married there. The frame was made from MDF and painted to look like wood by dry-brushing thinned brown paint over a yellow base. To finish it off, I filled the panels with a hemmed fabric.

I wanted to use colour to bring the room together and to introduce some warmth to the room. I picked out the warm red of the rug and used it for the curtains, new loose dining-chair covers and sofa cushions. Finally, we went outside to freshen up the balcony with a lick of paint and to rearrange the furniture. It was important that it looked like an added bonus, not just an afterthought.

BEFORE

kitchen

Unlike the rest of the apartment, the kitchen was certainly not magnolia or bland. The oranges, yellows and blues screamed at me to put my sunglasses back on. Richard tried to excuse it by explaining that the units and work surface were there when they arrived. His choice of flooring and wall colour had been an attempt to tie the look together. He was right. Orange is a very difficult colour to work with but, in my opinion, he'd have been better off getting rid of the lot and starting from scratch. Those colours were very dated, made the room look even smaller and took away from the view. Something drastic had to be done to play up the positive points. Where I could I wanted to work with the natural colours of the seaside in this apartment. Painting the walls a light sky blue made the room larger and lighter. Richard turned out to be quite a handyman and easily replaced the garish flooring with a neutral wood laminate. Those nightmarish orange doors were covered with a cloud-white washable laminate that can be cut to size. All that remained was the view. I asked Erica to clean the windows so that it could at least be seen clearly. Then we

Erica
' I'd like to go to Ann's house to see just how clean her windows are '

AFTER

painted the balcony floor a golden sandy colour, which progressed naturally from the new kitchen floor and was a reminder of the beach nearby.

master bedroom

This was the most unprepossessing room in the apartment. 'Luxury'? You could have fooled me. That word creates a particular image in buyers' minds. They would be disappointed if they walked in to see something that shabby. The only thing that convinced me it was the master bedroom was the existence of an en suite bathroom. Otherwise, it was untidy and unimpressive.

I decided a luxurious feel could be achieved by a few simple measures – first of all by adding colour. Although Erica had her

AFTER

doubts about my choice of a pale chocolate or café au lait for the walls, I overrode them. She may never have seen anything like it in a bedroom before, but there's a first time for everything. The curtains were hung properly and tied back. Once we'd tidied away the piles of clothes, we discovered a sofa hidden underneath. It looked much happier once its burden was exchanged for a couple of sharp blue cushions. A new bedhead was added to give a more ritzy but formal impression. The key finishing touches were the new bedding and cushions, a couple of pictures above the bed and a plant in the window. Hey presto! The room was transformed.

Turning my attention to the en suite bathroom, I felt the lino looked as if it was in a country cottage. It was not expensive to replace the lino with a marble lookalike laminate floorcovering, which looked a million dollars. The blue accent colour from the bedroom was repeated on the walls. Then it was just a question of putting away old bathrobes and towels and adding unused soaps and fluffy towels to give it that much-needed ambience.

AFTER

> Richard
> It looks better
> than any cruise
> ship I've
> been on

second bedroom

It was advertised as a second bedroom but there was one thing missing – a bed. Other than that, the room had been used as a dumping ground. It was a mess. What's more, it was waving a dangerous red flag to a prospective buyer: an area of damp had been fixed but not repainted. In a buyer's mind, that could signal the thought that other less visible things might have been neglected, too. Obviously this room had to be transformed from an abandoned junk room into a bedroom. Getting rid of the mess and installing a bed was not enough. I plumped for a bright sunny yellow colour for the walls with fine yellow curtains with white muslin underneath so the sun could stream through while a sense of intimacy was retained. Taking inspiration from the natural colours of the carpet and walls, I hung pictures carefully and invested in new bedlinen and cushions. The finishing touch was the vase of daffodils, which completed the pleasant spring-like atmosphere of the room.

By the time I'd finished, Richard and Erica were 100 per cent convinced that their hard work had been worthwhile. Their apartment was presented to look as if it was worth the asking price and would provide a luxury lifestyle for any prospective buyer. I did spend a little more than perhaps I normally would on a project of this type but, remember, luxury doesn't come cheap. When I left, Richard and Erica were expecting an offer soon.

COST	
Paint	£149
Flooring	£165
including Vision flooring in kitchen, Gerflor, £15 per pack	
Accessories	£1,030
including double duvet cover, Bedeck, £70	
'Caversham' headboard, MFI, £109	
'Provence' pillowcase, Peacock Blue, £10.50 each flexible laminate, Elescoflex, £29 per roll	
Labour	£430
TOTAL	£1,774

Erica

I wasn't sure about the colours at the beginning but now I'm really impressed

AFTER
viewers' comments

'Now you notice the view from the kitchen. Before you were distracted by the clash of colours.'

'The colours make a big difference to all the rooms. They open them out.'

'Before, you felt as if you wanted to get out of the door fairly quickly. Now you want to stay longer.'

how to

CARE FOR WOODEN FLOORS

Flooring has a tremendous impact on a room. Whether in a traditional or sleek contemporary setting, wooden flooring imparts a natural warmth and style of its own. By definition, it suffers an enormous amount of wear and tear from everyday use from shoes, furniture or spillages, so it is essential to look after it well if it is to retain its good looks.

treating minor damage

Before treating any minor damage, find out how the boards have been treated. The traditional finishes of oil and wax are the easiest to repair because they make it relatively straightforward to get to the wood. Superficial damage can usually be remedied by rubbing in paste wax with extra-fine wire wool. If the damage is a result of pressure from heavy furniture, try covering it with a damp cloth, then ironing it. The hot moisture should encourage the wood fibres to expand to their original shape. Keep stiletto heels at bay at all costs.

A polyurethane finish is harder to damage, but any damage is also harder to treat. First lightly sand the area without cutting into the wood itself. Gently wipe away any dust. Use a paint pad to apply the new polyurethane and thin out towards the edges with a dry brush. Water-based polyurethane gives a clear finish, while oil-based polyurethane will darken with age.

restoring an original floor

If you have discovered a wooden floor under an old carpet, more drastic action will probably be needed. Do not underestimate the amount of work it will take to achieve a really sound attractive finish. Call in the professionals if you have doubts about your own staying power. First sink any loose nails, secure loose boards or replace rotten ones. If the floor is in really good condition, you may be able to get away with sanding by hand, but more likely you will need to hire a sanding machine and an edge sander to take off accumulated dirt, worn paint or polish. This is a noisy and dirty job and will take some time. Vacuum up the resulting dust and clean the boards with white spirit.

Treating floors

Once stripped, there are a number of treatments to choose from – paint, varnish or woodstain. Whichever finish you choose, you can be sure that it will be a lasting, natural solution that will add value to your home.

Sealing

Unless the floor is painted, it will need sealing properly for protection. Among the various sealants available there are oils, waxes and, most popular, polyurethane. A properly sealed floor should be easy to clean, needing only a good sweep or vacuum and a wipe with a damp mop. Try to avoid getting it too wet. Long-term maintenance may be a little more troublesome. An oiled or waxed finish will probably need to be renewed after a couple of months. A sealed floor has a much longer life but if it begins to get a bit worn it may need refinishing to prevent the wood being damaged by dirt and moisture.

Painting

Before painting, be sure to prime the floor well before using a hard-wearing gloss, floor or deck paint. Primer is not necessary if you are liming the floor. If liming, give the floor a good scrub with a dry brush to open up the grain, work the liming agent (white paint, liming wax or gesso) into the wood with steel wool, wipe away any surplus then seal with polyurethane. Staining is another option that does not require a primer but remember to use several coats of varnish for a really hard, protective finish.

FABRIC-COVERED SCREEN

Transform a screen that has seen better days into a
feature that will add a touch of class to any room

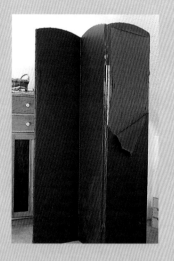

What you need

- panelled screen
- tailor's chalk
- scissors
- fabric and matching
  thread
- tape measure
- iron-on hemming
- pins and safety pins
- staple gun
- rope (for handles)
- braid
- hammer and brass
  upholstery nails
- screwdrivers and
  screws
- hinges and small
  screw-in brass
  castors
- pictures for framing

1 Separate and strip the screen's panels. Cut
two contrasting fabric pieces per panel, each
1.5cm (⅝in) larger all round than the panel.
Make sure any patterns match across the panels
and that motifs are centred.
Frame: Cut a 35cm (14in) fabric square with a
23cm (9in) square 'window'. Cut 1cm (⅜in)
diagonals at the 'window' corners.

2 Turn a 1.5cm (⅝in) hem round the 'window'
and fix with iron-on hemming. Press a 1.5cm (⅝in)
hem round the outside edges. Fix one (top edge)
with hemming. Pocket: Cut a 36 x 26cm (14¼ x
10¼in) rectangle of fabric and hem. Stitch along
one long edge (opening) to strengthen. Machine
stitch required number of pockets and frames on
to the fabric panels, leaving top edges open.

3 Turn under the edges of the large fabric pieces before stapling to the panels. Stretch the fabric outwards from the centre for a smooth fit.

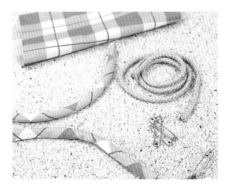

4 Handles: Cut two 4 x 20cm (1½ x 8in) strips of fabric. Fold in half lengthways, right sides facing. Sew a 5cm (2in) seam down the longer side. Turn the right side out. Pull an 18cm (7in) length of rope through each 'tube', using a safety pin to help.

5 Fix braid to cover the edges, evenly spacing the nails. Start from the midpoint on the bottom edge of each panel. Turn in the raw ends of the handles, attach them to the outside edges of the outside panels. Lay the panels flat. Attach hinges and castors. Slide pictures into the fabric frames.

CLAPHAM

Two-bedroom basement
flat with large living
room/kitchen/diner,
compact bathroom,
separate toilet. South-
facing garden.
£199,950.

Some of the most desirable property can be found in Clapham, a district of London just south of the Thames. Clapham's main attractions are its vast common, its good transport links to the West End and the City and the excellent locations for property.
It has become so popular with couples and young families that it has earned its nickname of 'Nappy Valley'. It is also popular with those who want to escape the buzz of the city but enjoy the café culture with its many bars, restaurants and delis. Good properties are at a premium here and tend to find new owners pretty smartish. However, Jonathan and Cathy's basement flat had been up for sale for ten long months. Whatever was wrong with it?

Jonathan was a solicitor while Cathy was the office manager at a photographic library. They had lived in their flat for six years with their two cats and had reached the point where they wanted to move to somewhere bigger. They thought that their lack of success in selling the place might be down to the fact that they hadn't maintained it consistently over the years, the carpet had seen better days and both the bathroom and kitchen looked rather dated. Cathy seemed fairly phlegmatic about the situation, unconcerned that viewers might not like the flat but confident that eventually someone would come along and recognise its potential. The question was, how long would that be?

Visiting it for the first time, I was immediately struck by the underwhelming welcome. The front door was down an alley at the side of the house where, straight in front of me, a dustbin blocked the route to the garden. Apart from the dark and cluttered hall, there was a very strong smell of cat everywhere. However fond owners may be of their pets, a buyer almost certainly will not appreciate the prospect of inheriting any distinctive odour. The flat itself was pretty neglected and needed new carpets throughout. Every single room needed work and created the impression that to put it all right would incur considerable extra expense above the asking price. Typical buyers in this part of London would not want to pay top dollar and then have to shell out another £20,000 in renovation costs. If Jonathan and Cathy wanted to sell their home at all, I felt that the whole place needed a radical overhaul. Cathy felt her home was comfortable but to an outsider it looked anything but. I wanted to get rid of the carpet and the smell of the cats, to finish off all the DIY jobs, reorganise the kitchen and living room, and completely redefine the bedroom. To transform this sadly neglected flat into a bijou London pad, it would need all hands on deck.

Doctor's Diagnosis

To make the flat more modern we had to:

- Declutter and decorate the hall
- Reorganise the living room and kitchen
- Change the carpet
- Revamp the bathroom
- Redefine and refit the bedroom
- Add up-to-date details

BEFORE
viewers' comments

'You'd have to redo the whole of the kitchen and bathroom.'

'My first impression was that it stank of cats – hideous.'

'It needs new carpets everywhere.'

'Every room you see, you just think more money, more money, more money.'

AFTER

entrance

Apart from moving the dustbin, I felt that more needed to be done to make the approach to the flat more attractive. We framed the glimpse of garden by erecting a small trellis pergola and hung small pots of primroses and daffodils from it. A touch as small as that can make all the difference to first impressions, making buyers approach the flat in a positive frame of mind.

To keep them feeling that way, something drastic needed to be done in the hallway. Keeping a bicycle in such a small space makes it seem even smaller. Blocking the passage by hanging too many coats there was not helping either. I was determined to keep Jonathan and Cathy's gorgeous framed poster of tropical fish, though I was less sure about the turquoise wall colour, which had become scuffed and dirty in places. Sure enough, we repainted the hallway in a neutral shade and rehung the poster where it could be seen more clearly. The carpet was replaced with a wood-effect floor and the radiator was boxed in with a trellis radiator cover. A plant and a shiny round mirror provided those all-important finishing touches. That's all it took to open out the space and make it seem much lighter, brighter and, most importantly, inviting.

living/dining/kitchen

Typical of many London basement conversions, two rooms had been knocked through to give a lighter open-plan living area and kitchen. It should have looked quite spacious but, instead, it looked cramped and messy. The tatty desk groaning under Jonathan's DJ decks and hi-fi equipment didn't make a great focal point in the room. The first thing that needed to be done was to give the place a really good clean. In fact, the kitchen

AFTER

was efficient and compact, although there was a lot of under-utilised space on the walls while the surfaces were over-utilised with old pots and pans and clutter covering the worktops. Worst of all, I was appalled when one of the couple's cats made its way in through a cat-flap in the window and over the counter. How unhygienic was that? The security grilles across the windows added nothing aesthetically.

A warm neutral colour on the walls did its usual trick of unifying the whole room and making it seem larger and lighter. Using the same wood-effect flooring used in the hall enhanced the new sense of space, too. I brought the sitting area together by placing a deep blue rug under the occasional tables in front of the sofa and by using some scatter cushions in ochre and blue. A striking focal point was provided by a fantastic boxed shelving unit that extended right to the ceiling. It really gave the room a more modern feel that it didn't have before. It was used to house some of Jonathan's hi-fi equipment and some judiciously arranged books and treasures.

The kitchen was given a new lease of life by painting the dark brown unit doors with special melamine paint to give a more modern look with minimum effort and expense. The walls were painted the same colour as those in the living area to unify the space. Adding some new shelving and cabinets also helped bring it up to date. The offending cat-flap and security grilles were disguised behind split-cane blinds. As usual, I wanted to define the dining area by laying the table invitingly, using fresh daffodils as a centrepiece.

Both halves of the room were given a really thorough clean, which began to rid the house of the cat smell even if I couldn't get rid of the cats themselves. I was extremely pleased with the way the room had become neater, tidier and much bigger.

BEFORE

bathroom

The bathroom and separate toilet virtually left me speechless. This was no way to show these intensely private spaces. As they were, no one would be tempted to stay in them for longer than they had to. I was intrigued by Cathy's remark that 'Surely a bath's to clean you, not for you to clean', but I totally disagreed. If a bathroom doesn't look spotless, you'll lose money on your sale. The bathroom was small and, frankly, didn't look too hygienic. The bath and basin were distinctly uninviting. Even with a good clean, the limescale and general wear and tear remained evident. The only solution was to use a specialist bathroom re-enamelling kit, a cheap and quick alternative to buying a whole new suite. I brought in some modern rubber floorcovering, cleaned up the grouting and painted the walls a soothing aqua and the wood ceiling white. Then it was simply a question of dressing the room with bathmats, towels and accessories to match.

The toilet may have been small but it was the source of the worst smell. One of the cats used it too! So it was up with the carpet and in with the rubber floorcovering. A fresh coat of paint on the walls, ceiling and woodwork, a friendly plant and a picture on the cistern made all the difference. But what really transformed the room was the exhaustive cleaning it got.

AFTER

master bedroom

The bedroom was painted a hot tangerine. I thought some buyers would respond more positively to a more inoffensive cornflower blue. The bed was on the floor, giving the strong impression that this was a student's room, and the doors on the ugly mirrored wardrobe were falling off. Jonathan was horrified when we began to take the wardrobe to pieces, unconvinced that there was a better alternative. I chose sea grass matting for the floor – a light and natural finish, that always looks good. Replacing the ugly radiator with a modern vertical one was another radical change. It not only made a bold statement and looked like a piece of artwork in its own right, it had the added bonus of freeing up some wall space for a mirror

> **Cathy**
> When we moved in, we did have great vision but it didn't happen

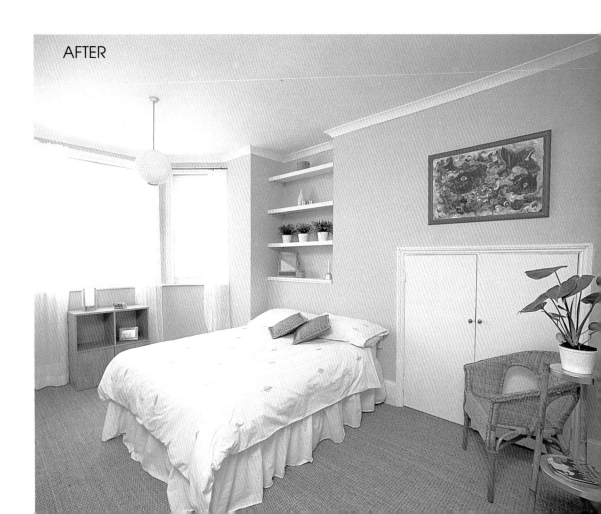

AFTER

and a plant stand. Storage was at a premium in here, but by lifting the bed from the floor, space was created beneath it, as well as in a new freestanding wardrobe. I had the lower shelves of the alcove boxed in so the bed would fit better, leaving some of the shelves open above it. Moving the furniture around made a tremendous difference, again giving the feeling that the room had become larger. The windows were re-dressed with cool white blinds and thin muslin hangings, the bay providing a convenient home for another small shelf/cupboard unit for storage. At last, the room felt clean and pure – just the place anyone would want to spend time in.

second bedroom/study

The second bedroom had already been turned into a study. It was the least disturbing room in the flat and needed only the minimum of change. The walls were painted the same colour as the bathroom, and we

AFTER

used the same sea grass floorcovering as in the bedroom. Another cubed storage unit came in handy for storage above the desk. Properly cleaned and tidied, it gave the impression of being a slick and efficient workplace.

It had been hard work but the results were spectacular. Jonathan and Cathy were happy with the results and even thought they might make that desired sale sooner rather than later. Sure enough, the cost of the transformation was covered when they accepted an offer £5,000 above the asking price!

```
COST
Paint                          £110
Flooring                       £605
Storage units                  £760
Accessories                    £611
  including
  radiator cover,
  Jali, £142
Labour                         £500
TOTAL                        £2,586
```

AFTER
viewers' comments

'It's exactly the sort of place I'm looking for.'

'I'm sure someone will love it and they'll get the asking price.'

Jonathan
It looks a different flat – a big improvement

how to

USE PLANTS DECORATIVELY

Plants and flowers can add life, colour and contrast to a room, but only if they are healthy and displayed well. Unless you are blessed with green fingers, it is wise to choose plants that will withstand almost any amount of neglect. Take advice from the local garden centre. When choosing a plant, make sure that it looks healthy, that roots are not coming out of the pot's drainage holes and that there is no moss or slime on the compost.

caring for plants

Houseplants come in all shapes and sizes to suit almost any situation. The rules of thumb when caring for indoor plants are: put them where they will thrive best, not only where they look best; water and feed them according to instructions; treat any disease or pest the moment you spot it; avoid extremes of cold and heat; trim off dead flowers and leaves; if a plant begins to look as if it is suffering, ask yourself why it is suffering and remedy it. Find out what conditions your plants experience in the wild and try to imitate them as closely as possible in terms of compost, light, temperature and water.

choosing containers

There is no limit to the type of containers suitable for houseplants. There is no reason why you can't use decorative tins, seaside buckets, teapots, glass containers or even an old butler's sink. The most common container of course is the tried-and-tested terracotta pot, which goes well with any plant and allows moisture to evaporate through its sides. Such pots can be used alone or placed inside a cache-pot whose design suits the décor better. Groups of plants can make an attractive feature or focal point in a room. They may be freestanding, or smaller arrangements will fit into terrariums, bottle gardens or a trough. Window boxes do not have to be restricted to the outside of the house. If there's no sill or they are in danger of falling, try bringing them inside. They may be ideal for growing herbs or small flowering border plants.

Use your imagination to find ways of using plants to enhance a space, be it dramatic, exotic, soothing or just plain welcoming. Remember, a few well chosen, well cared-for plants are an asset to any décor; an overgrown jungle is a definite liability.

what plant goes where?

Small, bushy flowering pot plants such as chrysanthemums, azaleas or cyclamen make good seasonal centrepieces for tables, and will also sit happily on a mantelpiece or windowsill. They can be difficult to keep alive after they have flowered and are often transplanted into the garden. Trailing plants such as the spider plant, sweetheart plant, wandering Jew or devil's ivy can sit on a plant stand, shelf or wall bracket and cascade downwards. If placed near a window, they can be used to hide an unappealing view. The important thing to remember is that just because they're out of easy reach, they still need the same attention as any other plant or they will become leggy and miserable. Exotic palms make grand architectural statements. They suit both a modern minimalist environment and a busier more traditional room where they can be combined with other plants in an impressive display. They will live particularly happily in living or dining rooms where the temperature remains reasonably constant.

If you want to put greenery into your bathroom, try one of the ferns. They love a warm humid environment so if the bathroom doesn't steam up often, make sure you spray them regularly. Kitchens are generally not a great home for plants because of the fluctuating temperature. But if you insist, it's best to go for the real death-defying specimens such as peace lilies, sweetheart plants, mother-in-law's tongues, devil's ivy or umbrella plants. If you just want something small on the window ledge, try growing your own herbs.

ZINC CORNER TABLE

Turn dead space into a practical storage-bin-cum-table
with a contemporary twist in five easy steps

What you need

- pair of compasses and ruler
- paper and pencil
- scissors
- jigsaw and handsaw
- protective face mask
- 6mm (¼in) MDF
- paintbrush
- eggshell paint in chosen colour

- screwdriver and screws
- 10 furniture blocks
- lengths of batten
- sheet of hardboard
- perforated zinc sheeting
- 6 mirror-fixing screws with silver-
  coloured caps

1 To make a quadrant template, draw and cut out a paper circle and fold it twice. Check the quadrant fits your corner, adjust, then cut out. Using the template, cut three MDF quadrants, wearing a face mask for protection. Leave one whole (base); cut a hand hole in one (lid); remove centre of the third, leaving a 4cm (1½in) border all round (top frame for lid).

2 Paint the lid. While it is drying, fix the base in the corner by attaching it to the walls and floor. Use two furniture blocks on each straight edge and two on the curved edge to hold the front vertical battens.

3 Decide on the height of the table and cut two side battens to length. Screw them to the wall. Screw the remaining furniture blocks at the right height on the wall then fix the MDF top frame in position.

4 Cut two vertical battens to fit on the front edge of the table between the top and the base.

5 Cut a piece of hardboard to fit the front, adding 5cm to the height and allowing for the skirting. Cut the zinc to the same shape with an additional 2cm (¾in) all round. Place the zinc over the hardboard and fold over the extra. Fix to the battens with mirror-fixing screws. Put the lid on top.

COLCHESTER

Attractive three-bedroom detached house in south Colchester with large living/dining room, compact kitchen, bathroom, large garden. Ample parking space. £123,995.

Colchester is the oldest recorded town in English history and is surrounded by the countryside made famous by the painter John Constable. It boasts a castle built on the foundations of a Roman temple, several museums and a Roman wall. Yet the town also has a modern and sophisticated side providing good shopping, restaurants and a thriving nightlife. This combination of old and new makes it irresistible. Only 62 miles from London, Colchester has two train stations and a bus station keeping it well connected with the rest of the country.

Property in this desirable neck of the woods usually attracts a stampede of buyers but one house had been on the market for over four months without raising any interest. It belonged to Graham, a sales manager for a nationwide builders' merchant, and his wife, Carolyn, a childminder trainer. They were desperate to sell their house because they had found their dream home and were anxious not to lose it. They were genuinely mystified as to why they hadn't had any interested buyers although they were beginning to suspect it might just have something to do with their choice of colour scheme.

When I first walked in, my head span. The living room was a riot of patterns, pinks and reds. It was overwhelming. Every room downstairs had the same claustrophobic effect. To me, this was an example of very personal and extreme English taste. The house was making a strong statement that would not necessarily be everyone's cup of tea. Apart from the bright colours, jangling patterns leapt from the carpets, wallpaper border, furniture fabric, wall stencils, lace curtains, teapot collection and general clutter. Graham's, shall we say 'interesting' contribution came in the form of photographic posters – quite a contrast in style. Even their ten-year-old son Luke had more games than he could possibly need stored in the second bedroom-cum-office. Everything needed to be toned down if a buyer was to feel calm and at home. Only then would he or she be able to focus on the house itself and how it might be adapted to suit other furniture and colour schemes. If Graham and Carolyn wanted to get their dream home, they would have to be prepared to compromise in their decoration of this one first.

Fortunately, they had begun to get the message and were willing to follow my lead. I decided to concentrate on the downstairs rooms and the bedroom-cum-office. The other rooms were being presented perfectly well.

Doctor's Diagnosis

To calm the house down we had to:
- Depersonalise and declutter
- Get rid of the girliness
- Close in the stairs and build storage underneath
- Create space

BEFORE
viewers' comments

'It really looks like an Indian restaurant back in the 1970s.'

'You only get the idea that someone's colour blind.'

'You go into the lounge – nightmare. You go into the dining room – nightmare. Upstairs, the bedrooms are a nightmare as well.'

'It feels claustrophobic with too many things.'

BEFORE

living

This was quite simply a case of creating a pleasant neutral setting with nothing in it to which the buyer could object. The swirling patterned red carpet was shown the skip and in came a chic new beige-coloured substitute. The walls were painted a soft clean colour to obliterate the pinks, the border and even the stencils so lovingly done by Carolyn. I did allow another border back into the room but it was much more discreet than the last and served to break up the bare expanses of wall. It was backed with adhesive so rolled into place quite easily.

I removed the busy net curtains, but because Graham and Carolyn valued their privacy I hung some unobtrusive sheer fabric there instead. We hid the area under the stairs with a decent door rather than an old sheet and installed some neat storage systems inside so it didn't look quite so much like a dumping ground. I felt that Graham's choice of artwork might offend some people so replaced it with something more innocuous. Graham's building expertise came in handy as he boxed in the open stairs with MDF and demolished the stair gates before we could run up the brand-new carpet. Finally, the furniture was rearranged so the room didn't look so crowded.

AFTER

Carolyn
I'm known as the dizzy blonde who lives in the pink house

dining

The dining room was a repeat of all the same mistakes committed in the living room – more of those pinks bringing the space in on the occupants. The dining table was tucked under the window as if it was never used, with the result that it looked as if it was fighting for space to be there at all. The surfaces were jammed with the family's treasures including many family photos. Too many personal possessions on display in a house can distract the buyer from the business in hand so they had to be put in storage until a new home was found for them. The first casualty was the teapot

Carolyn
We're starting to think it's too pink

AFTER

collection. Out of 38, Carolyn was allowed to keep seven favourites to be displayed so they could be individually admired.

We took down the shelves, leaving one as a feature to hold some plants. The walls and floors received the same treatment as the living room so the entire area looked cooler, uncluttered and calm. The table was reinstated in the centre of the room with a simple runner and potted plant as decoration. I chose an orchid because they need little attention and last for ages.

The cabinet looked much better with only a small selection of ornaments on display, while the greatest find of all was the antique drinks cabinet lurking unnoticed behind the front door. I had liberated the space for it to be displayed just where it belonged. Finally I decided to leave the curtains alone. No longer lost in the maze of different colours, they looked perfectly attractive and added just the right touch of life to the room.

BEFORE

kitchen

The kitchen suffered from being painted an even more vivid sickly pink than the rest of the downstairs rooms. It was the site of Carolyn's first venture into stencilling and, carried away by her initial success, she had gone mad and stencilled everywhere. But not for much longer. Apart from showing off her taste too clearly, they looked rather dated. Fresh green proved a much more

AFTER

suitable kitchen colour and with a good clean and a bit of surface clearing, it looked perfect. The only other thing I wanted to do was utilise the breakfast bar standing sadly in a corner. It wasn't expensive to buy two stools and then lay the table with mats and glasses that tied in with the new colour scheme.

Graham
After all the stick I've taken from Ann over the pink, that's it. It's banned. It's too girly, too feminine. No more

second bedroom/office

BEFORE

I decided to turn the second bedroom-cum-office into a definitive office. All Luke's games were carted into the garden where he sportingly agreed that the majority of them could go to charity. Then it was time to get to work on the room itself. The removal of the games had released some more space. Then it was just a case of making the room look less busy by eliminating the wallpaper under a coat of restful blue paint toning with the existing curtains and carpet. A general tidy of the desk and chest of drawers, and the admittance of a small bookcase with carefully arranged books immediately gave the impression of an efficient workplace. Should the work become too tiring, there was always the daybed. I felt this looked better with a new cover in a muted orange. The jolly blue scatter cushions tied the

AFTER

whole thing in with the rest of the room. Just in case it looked too sterile, I added some plants, fresh flowers and a couple of ornaments for interest.

My two initially reluctant helpers were won over – so much so that Graham was threatening never to let Carolyn choose a pink colour scheme again. Although it hurt her to lose her precious stencils and beloved teapot collection, she was ready to admit that the place was vastly improved. That dazzling chintzy look had been replaced by a cool canvas against which they could show off a few of their prized possessions. But more importantly, they had paved the way for a buyer to begin to imagine what it might be like to move in there with his or her own things. As they worked, Graham and Carolyn were driven forward by the idea of their dream home waiting for them. Sure enough, their house was sold for £1,500 over the asking price immediately after I left them.

COST	
Paint	£411
Carpet	£746
The Carpet Foundation, £315.25 per square metre	
Accessories	£541
including antique pine stools, Argos, £26.99 per pair	
Readyroll border, HA Interiors, £6.49 per roll	
Labour	£200
TOTAL	£1,898

Graham
I should think buyers will be over the moon

AFTER
viewers'
comments

'You get a totally different feeling now. It looks so much bigger.'

'Light, sunny and much more tasteful.'

'Last time it would have been "no", but now I think it's quite nice.'

'It's much more saleable now, something you'd want to buy.'

how to

PAINT INTERIORS

Painting a room can transform its character. Make sure you choose the right finish to give the results you want. Matt emulsions absorb light to give a soft, flat finish, providing a good background for most rooms. At the other end of the scale, gloss paints reflect light and provide a hard-wearing finish, usually for woodwork. Between these is a range of eggshells and vinyl silks, all of which reflect light in varying degrees.

which colour?

The colour you choose can make a huge difference to the perception of a room. Pale colours tend to make the walls and ceiling seem to recede, making the space seem bigger and airier. The shiny finishes of gloss, eggshell and vinyl silk reflect the light to make a room look even larger. If you're still battling for space use a monochrome colour scheme throughout the room – off-whites, beiges and taupes – and it will seem larger still. Dark colours make the walls close in, making the space more intimate. Matt finishes will make it seem smaller, too.

If the room is too tall, make the ceiling seem lower by painting it a darker colour than the walls. The illusion of lowering it further can be achieved by extending the darker ceiling colour on to the upper portion of the wall. Mark the start point with masking tape in order to get a straight, clean dividing line. How far down the wall you paint is a matter of choice. It might be only as far as a picture rail or, in the absence of one, it may be the top quarter of the wall.

If your room seems too squat, get rid of all horizontal lines such as picture rails, borders or dados and paint vertical stripes on the walls. Even the most subtle differentiation between stripes will be enough to make the room grow. Painting the ceiling a pale colour will make it seem higher.

Remember that colour can profoundly influence mood, so it is important to select the right palette for the feeling you want and to choose the proportions well. Colour is an immensely personal thing and our reactions to it are generally subjective. White is clean, calming and peaceful. Red has connotations with passion. Blue can seem cool, while yellow is viewed as a sunny, upbeat colour. Selling your house demands the choice of soft neutrals precisely so they do not intrude into a buyer's consciousness, unduly distracting or unsettling him or her.

When choosing the colours for a room, also
bear in mind the amount of natural light in there. In
the cold English light, for example, it is often better
to use slightly warmer colours to bring the room to
life – off-white or cream is often better than pure
white, while soft aquamarines, eau de Nile,
peaches and apricots are better than bright blues or
oranges. Also look at the proposed colour during
different times of the day and under artificial light.
You may need to adjust the lighting in a room (see
How to make the most of lighting, page 118) to
ensure that it doesn't become too dull.

wise decision-making

Choose colours carefully, taking into account whatever furnishings may already exist in the room. Tiny squares of colour on paint charts are not representative of what the colour will look like on all four walls. If possible, paint a large piece of lining paper or MDF and move it around the room so you can see exactly how it looks in different lights at different times of the day. Think about when the room is used most often and judge whether or not this is when the colour looks its best. When you have finally made your decision, it's time to get down to the hard work of actually painting.

Essential equipment

- Assorted household paintbrushes/roller/paint pad
- Assorted grades of sandpaper
- Filler
- Filling knife
- Radiator paintbrush
- Radiator roller
- Rag
- Bucket and sponge

preparation

Make sure all odd jobs are completed before painting. Fixing a sash cord or a broken door or light switch later will mess up your finished paintwork. Remove furniture from the room or stack it in the centre and cover with a dustsheet. Ensure the surfaces to be painted are clean and carefully prepared, repairing any damage such as blisters, flaking paint, chips and cracks.

technique

Get the right amount of paint on your brush by dipping it into the paint until one-third of the bristles are covered, then pressing it against the paint container. If using a roller, push it backwards and forwards in the paint tray, then up the slope of the tray to get rid of the excess paint. As you work, make sure the paint is 'laid off', or smoothed over, while wet. Remember that two thin coats of paint are better than one thick one.

The best order to paint a room is · ceiling, walls, then woodwork.

Painting techniques

Painting is not difficult, but for best results the technique used should be adapted slightly according to the nature of the place that is being painted

Painting a ceiling

If using a brush, begin in a corner near the window then work in half-metre strips away from the light. Lay off after roughly every metre (yard). If using a roller, first paint the corners the roller cannot reach with a small brush then cover the main area to be painted with alternating diagonal strokes. Lay off with strokes parallel to one of the walls.

Painting woodwork

When painting a door with a flat surface, paint from the top to bottom in strips making sure you work fast enough to prevent the paint hardening before the section next to it hardens. If painting a panelled door, paint the panels first, working from either side to meet in the middle. Then paint the sections between them before finishing off with the top, bottom then sides of the door.

Apply masking tape to the edges of windows and begin painting the sections nearest the glass, working outwards to paint the window frame last. Pull the top of a sash window down and the bottom up before painting. Paint the meeting rail first then as much as possible of the bottom window and the top. Paint inside the top of the frame and 50cm (20in) down the outside runners. Almost close the window and paint the top 50cm (20in) of the inside runners and finish in the same order as the sash window.

Painting a wall

Start your brushwork at the top corner of a wall and work in strips down to the skirting board before returning to the top. Use a smaller brush to 'cut in' around the doors and windows. A roller should be used in alternating diagonal strokes so that the gaps and joining lines are properly merged. Try to paint a wall while working in the same light so that you can see exactly where you have covered. Be sure to open windows and have adequate ventilation while avoiding drafts straight on to the paint itself. Make sure that you complete a wall before knocking off for the night, otherwise the line where you stopped then restarted will be noticeable.

Painting a radiator

Always paint radiators when they are cold and do not turn the heating on again until the paint is dry. Use a small brush and a crevice roller for the tricky areas. If the paint runs, pimples or blisters, then leave to dry thoroughly, sand it back, clean the surface and repaint.

HANDY WORK SPACE

Some clever planning is all that is needed to convert a small space into a functional workstation

inside a wardrobe

What you need

- wooden wardrobe
- pencil and ruler
- screwdriver, wood screws and small chipboard screws
- 8 small right-angled brackets
- handsaw
- 2.4m (2½yd) of 17 x 25mm (¹¹⁄₁₆ x 1in) softwood batten
- 2 shelves of 18mm MDF cut to fit wardrobe
- electric drill and assorted drill bits
- 2.4m (2½yd) of 6 x
- 18mm (¼ x ¹¹⁄₁₆in) softwood batten
- large bulldog clips
- wastepaper bin
- document rack
- paintbrush
- eggshell paint
- 7 magazine files
- 12mm (½in) M6 roofing bolts
- nuts and bolts
- keyboard drawer
- noticeboard
- double-sided mirror pads
- printer tidy
- foldaway stool

1 Use right-angled brackets and thick battening to make two shelf supports inside the wardrobe, one 38cm (15in) from the top, the other at a comfortable desk height. Slide in the shelves. Drill a hole in the side/back of the wardrobe for cables to exit.

2 Cut six thin battens, 36cm (14¼in) long. Drill a hole at each end. In four, drill holes where the bulldog clips will sit. In the centre of one, drill two holes 3cm (1¼in) apart for a wastepaper bin. In the last, drill holes to match the pre-drilled holes on the document rack.

3 Paint the battens and the fronts of the magazine files. Put the files on the top shelf when dry.

4 Use roofing bolts to attach the bulldog clips and document rack to their battens. Drill holes in the bin 3cm (1¼in) apart close to the top of the bin. Attach it to its batten using nuts and bolts. Screw the battens on to the door.

5 Fit the keyboard drawer beneath the desk shelf, following the manufacturer's instructions. Fix the noticeboard above the bulldog clips using mirror pads.

6 Put your computer equipment in place and store a foldaway stool in the cupboard.

under the stairs

The space under stairs is often under-utilised. It may be ideal for converting into a compact office. A table, a chair and some innovative storage systems are all that is needed. Look at the space carefully and make sure every bit is used efficiently, right down to the areas under the highest and lowest steps. Think about the kind of lighting that will best illuminate the area. If you find it hard to keep your paperwork under control or want a degree of privacy, consider adding doors or a screen to shut the area off from view.

STOKE-ON-TRENT

Grade II listed
Victorian villa with
five bedrooms, two
reception rooms,
kitchen, bathroom. Close
to city centre.
£148,000.

Stoke-on-Trent is the heartland of the potteries. Royal Doulton, Minton, Wedgwood and Spode are among the numerous working factories. Stoke has a busy city centre with most of the major high street stores, a lively market, the Potteries Shopping Centre and the Festival Park, which includes attractions such as a multiplex cinema, Superbowl, water roller coaster and even a ski centre. There are plenty of cafés and restaurants and even a local speciality – the Staffordshire oatcake. A number of Victorian parks grace the city but if you want fresh air and exercise, it's only a short distance to the Staffordshire Moorlands and the Peak District National Park. The city is close to junctions 15 and 16 of the M6 and only about an hour's drive to Birmingham and Manchester airports or a 50-minute train ride from London. At one time it relied on mining and industry but both have declined over the last two decades and, with them, the property market.

However, there was one house that should have been snapped up but had remained on the market for almost two years. It belonged to Jo, who lived there with her two grown-up children, Nina and Joseph. She was finding the maintenance of a house that size never-ending and felt that the time had come for them to move on and for it to be occupied by a young family again. My job was to help them solve the mystery of why this large, comfortable family home wasn't attracting offers.

From the outside, the house looked as if it had plenty of character and would be eminently desirable. But the inside left a lot to be desired. As with many Victorian houses, the hall was dark but it was also very cramped and uninviting. Things went from bad to worse. Although the living room had recently been redecorated, the rest of the house was strewn with clutter and had certainly seen better days. The master bedroom had been turned into Joseph's pad while the others were at best crowded and at worst completely neglected. The whole house needed rescuing if it was to give the impression of being the sophisticated period home implied by the exterior. But where to begin?

Nina
I like my room as it is. It's full of personality

Doctor's Diagnosis

To restore period elegance and charm we had to:
- Lighten and brighten the hall
- Minimise the ugly kitchen wall
- Declutter the dining room and dress it
- Reinstate the master bedroom
- Rediscover the walls in Nina's room
- Rescue the abandoned turret room

BEFORE
viewers' comments

'It obviously hasn't had anything done to it for a long time.'

'You think they could have tidied up slightly.'

'Going into the kitchen's like walking into a crypt.'

'It's so untidy and the décor definitely wants changing.'

'You can't see the room for the stuff.'

AFTER

entrance

It's true that Victorian hallways tend to be dark but this one was unfriendly, too. The floor tiles that were lost under accumulated grime were restored to their former glory by giving them a scrub with an acid solution before sealing. The old dark carpet was replaced with a light mushroom shade and the walls were painted an elegant cream. Pot plants lent life, colour and contrast.

AFTER

dining

The dining room was a big challenge. It contained junk, from typewriters to straw donkeys, hiding the magnificent table and chairs. I wanted to create an atmosphere to captivate buyers when they walked in. By making an antiquing glaze out of matt emulsion, I gave the room a richer antique feel. I sponged it on to the wallpaper, then wiped over it with a cloth to get the dual effect of a rosy colour underneath and yellowish one on top, which enhanced the tones of Jo's furniture. I got rid of the heaviest furniture so that the room's focus would be the table and chairs. Then I set the table with Jo's china and crystal.

Jo
The kitchen is a real transformation. The wall isn't in your face any more

kitchen/dining

Clutter was piled up all over the working end of the kitchen while the other end was an uninviting dining area with a brick wall housing the microwave and two ugly laminate cupboard doors. Adhesive cork tiles provided an up-to-the-minute replacement for the worn lino. Then the units were polished and a stylish bit of window dressing added.

Family tension mounted when Nina announced that she liked the wall because it was 'different'. Fortunately, Jo shared my view that it was obtrusive and uninviting, so I watered down one part emulsion with ten parts water to make a wash. After applying it, I rubbed it down so it merged into the general colour scheme. Simple wooden door frames were created around the cupboard doors for a traditional look and I removed the doors, applied adhesive mouldings and glossed them before replacing them. Now they looked like old panelled doors that belonged to the period of the house. Finally, I brought the room together with a colour scheme of coordinating green and yellow.

AFTER

master bedroom

Upstairs, things got worse. The biggest bedroom had been given over to Joseph, an archaeology student who had moved in all his belongings, including a tumble-dryer and some gym equipment, from his previous flat. In a property of this size, a buyer wants to see

AFTER

an impressive master bedroom. It demanded to be reinstated to its rightful role. Once Joseph had agreed to swap with his mother, we could get rid of his junk and restore the bedroom furniture to its rightful place. I chose a soft pink for the walls and new coordinating bedlinen. We bought a new headboard to look less dated and overpowering than the previous one and added the finishing touches of new bedding, cushions, a rug and a small pot of flowers by the bed. We had successfully redefined the room making it comfortable and welcoming without being too feminine.

Nina's bedroom

Nina's bedroom, on the other hand, was stuck in a teenage time warp. She thought it had personality. I thought it was a mess. She was 23 but it looked as if the room had stayed the same since she was five. She was eventually persuaded that changing it would help sell the house. Before we could paint, she had to strip it of all the posters, drawings, the cuddly toys and all the rest of her treasures. I consoled her by pointing out that she would have had to face this anyway when they came to move. That 'personality' prevented a buyer from seeing the room for what it was. Once it was stripped bare, we needed only to paint the upper part of the walls a forget-me-not blue and we had a presentable blank canvas against which a buyer could imagine his or her own belongings.

turret room

Another gloomy flight of stairs led to a turret room. The room contained a broken bed, an old mattress and boxes storing cutlery and glasses. An open-top tank dripped in a corner.

AFTER

Abandoning a room like this is the same as putting money on the table, then walking away from it. Drastic action was required. Adding a banister for safety and repairing the door made the approach more welcoming. We hid the tank with MDF doors. A warm blue and yellow colour scheme countered the low temperature and a new blind and light fitting were added. With new bedlinen that toned with the walls, the room was presented in a new light. It could now be a child's room, an au pair's room, a playroom, or just a getaway.

Between us we restored the villa's charm by defining rooms, decluttering and cleaning, and playing up its best features. Sure enough, an offer was received days later.

```
COST
Paint                    £140
Carpet                   £385
Cork tiles, Nicoline     £120
Accessories              £600
    including 'Staks'
    metal Venetian blind,
    Ikea, £12.50
  'Linara' double duvet
    cover, Colouroll, £50
    Victorian moulding kit,
    Focus Do It All, £15.99
    Cream devore voile
    fabric, Terry's Fabric
    Warehouse, £3.99 per metre
    Clear basic glaze,
    Crown Paints,
    £10.49 per litre
Labour                   £700

TOTAL                  £1,945
```

AFTER
viewers' comments

'We'd consider buying it now. It's a lot better than it was.'

'It's brighter, more welcoming and together.'

'It feels more Victorian.'

'Is this the same room?'

'Wow.'

how to

MAKE THE MOST OF LIGHTING

Light and shade will be crucial components in the design of your home. Used cleverly they can highlight and disguise good and bad features. Lighting is often overlooked in the planning of a room but remember it can change the atmosphere at the flick of a switch. The right lighting can bring a room alive or calm it down. It can be dramatic, soothing, romantic or just plain functional. It is up to you to set the tone.

natural lighting

Watch the direction of sunlight entering each room and see how its effect changes throughout the day. Your choice of colours and arrangement of furniture should take this into account. Kitchens and living rooms benefit from having as much light as possible encouraged into the room. Clean the windows. Pull back curtains so they don't obstruct the light flow. Use light colours on the walls and furniture. In darker rooms, use gloss on the woodwork and hang mirrors to reflect more natural light into the space.

artificial lighting

When planning the lighting in a room, you must think about the layout of the room, how it is used, the furniture and the kinds of light that will suit the style of the room. Remember to take safety into account. You don't want accidents arising from badly lit kitchens or bathrooms, or from people tripping over stray flexes.

Lighting types

The most effective, easy way to transform a room is by changing the lighting. Dimmer switches give more flexibility still

Ambient lighting

Every room needs ambient or background lighting. Steer clear of central pendant lights because they can cast a rather bleak unfriendly atmosphere. Ceiling downlighters or spotlights can be angled for the right effect and, if on a dimmer, can produce a practical bright light by day and a more soothing intimate mood by night. If they are wired in separate circuits, you can dim one area of a room but illuminate another, governing the focus of the evening. For example, you may want to forget about the kitchen and concentrate on the dining table then, after the meal, shift attention towards the sitting area without having to be reminded of the washing up. A different mood can be established by introducing subtle shadows. Table lights, standard lamps and wall lights can all be used to this effect. Wall lights or uplighters will wash the walls in a softer, more flattering glow.

Task lighting

You will need concentrated areas of light on work surfaces, desks, reading or sewing chairs. There are all sorts of spotlights on the market ideal for task lighting. You may prefer a desk lamp or a standard spotlight to light wherever you are working. Kitchen worktops can be lit by angled downlighters, halogen spotlights on tracks or fluorescent lights under the upper wall cabinets. Bathroom mirrors will need good lighting, too. Almost everyone needs a good bedside light.

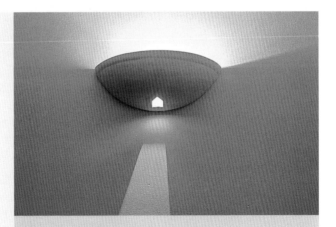

Dramatic lighting

You may also want lights to accentuate specific features in a room. Pictures, ornaments, plants or particular architectural features can all benefit from being in the spotlight. Lastly, flickering candles and firelight will completely change the ambience of the room. They convey a warmth, romanticism and sense of relaxation unlike any other.

TABLE STORAGE BOX

Let a modest wooden box take on a new identity
as a smart side table with invaluable
hidden storage space

What you need

- small wooden box
- screwdriver
- ruler or tape measure
- pencil
- paper
- handsaw
- 40mm x 40mm (1½ x 1½in) softwood batten
- clamp or workbench
- electric drill
- dowels

- chalk
- wood glue
- hammer
- jigsaw
- plywood panels
- scissors
- panel pins
- pine board
- medium-grade sandpaper
- 2 butt hinges and screws
- bradawl
- paintbrush
- woodwash

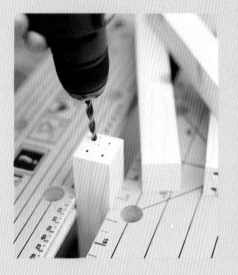

1 Remove and discard the box's handles, fixings and lid. Decide how high you would like the box to stand. Measure, mark and saw four appropriate lengths of batten for the legs. Place them vertically in a clamp and drill four holes in one end of each leg to hold the dowels.

2 Make four chalk marks on the bottom of the box in each corner, where the legs will go. Drill holes in the box base for the dowels. Squeeze wood glue into the holes in the box and legs. Insert a dowel into each hole in the legs and hammer each leg into position on the box. Do not stand the box on its legs until the glue is completely dry.

3 Using a jigsaw, cut ply panels big enough to fit all four sides from the top of the box to the floor. First shape a side panel by marking the position of the legs and the level of the bottom of the box. Draw a curve from the centre point to the base of one leg. Cut a paper pattern to match this curve and use to continue the curve to the other leg. Use the template on the other side panel. Repeat the process on the front and back panels.

4 Apply glue to the side edges of one of the ply side panels. Stick it to the box and legs, securing it with panel pins at regular intervals. Repeat with the other side panel, then the front and back panels.

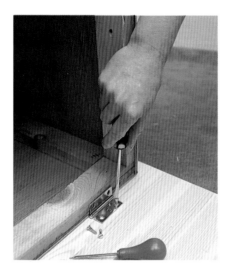

5 Cut a lid from the pine board, 3cm (1¼in) larger than the box all round. Sand smooth. Lay the box on its side next to the lid. Open the hinges and mark their positions on both the box and the lid. Make holes using a bradawl, then screw the hinges in place.

6 Apply woodwash to the box, both inside and out. Leave to dry.

The resulting table can be used in any number of different ways and in any number of different rooms. In the bedroom it may be used to store bulky clothes such as jumpers, or as an alternative to a laundry basket. It also makes a great bedside table.

In the living room, this piece will always be of use as a table and often as a place to store magazines and newspapers. Alternatively – especially when trying to sell your home and in the absence of a toy box – use it to hide any evidence that your living room doubles as a playroom. Dual-purpose furniture is particularly useful in a property where space is limited.

HAWKESBURY UPTON

Two-hundred-year-old two-bedroom house with two reception rooms, kitchen, bathroom, large garden and separate patio. £127,500.

Set deep in the heart of the picturesque Cotswolds, the village of Hawkesbury Upton has two big selling points. It is within easy access of the major towns of Cirencester, Cheltenham, Bristol and Bath, and is surrounded by beautiful rolling countryside. It is a prime commuter-belt location so houses tend to sell pretty fast but, unusually, Corner Cottage was alone in having been on the market for a record three months. Its owners, builder and sculptor Ken, and Emma, who works in the wine industry, had spent two very happy years there but had found their dream home only 100 yards up the road. They needed to sell the cottage fast if they were to clinch a deal.

The cottage itself was very quaint with ceilings so low that Ken conveniently acted as a cobweb brush because he was so tall. The approach was very attractive and I was expecting to enter a traditional 'olde English' cottagey home. Instead, I found something quite different. The front door opened directly into a living room crammed with books, furniture and sporting trophies. This charming old house was lost under the clutter. It was impossible to distinguish its best features. Much of the furniture was too big. Some of the pieces were impressive but dominated the rooms at the expense of everything else. Fortunately, not far away, was a barn where Emma and Ken kept their reject furniture. It seemed to me something of a treasure trove, not to mention a place for temporary storage. The stuffed animals were going to have to find another home for the time being. So, too, if I had my way, were the ferrets currently housed outside the kitchen window. I soon realised there would be a battle royal over them. Ken had vowed that under no circumstances was he going to move them and Emma was sticking by him. I decided to bide my time . . .

The thing that probably let the house down the most was the kitchen. I could only guess that Ken and Emma had run out of steam by the time they had got around to it. I've said more than once that all DIY jobs must be completed if you are hoping to sell your house. They only flag up to the buyer that there's work to be done the moment they move in. The yard was the other thing that failed to live up to its potential. Apart from being a home to the ferret cages – as far as I was concerned, that was enough to put anyone off – it didn't make you want to spend time there. I felt it could be turned into a superb outdoor room, which would add value to the house.

Doctor's Diagnosis

To reinvent the property as a country cottage we had to:
- Declutter the living and dining rooms
- Finish off the kitchen
- Tidy the yard
- Tidy the master bedroom
- Make the fire work

BEFORE
viewers' comments

'I like a cottage to look cottagey – and this doesn't.'

'It's the personification of countryside living – horses, dogs, shooting and killing things. It puts us townies off straight away.'

'The garden's lovely and has a cottagey feel but the rest of the house doesn't.'

BEFORE

living

I couldn't believe how much Ken and Emma had managed to cram into the living room. I soon established that the stuffed animals and hunting trophies weren't won by them, as 'countrified' as the couple claimed to be. I felt strongly that all these things might alienate many viewers. It's much easier to put them into temporary storage than run the risk of creating a negative approach to the house. Furniture was jammed into the room with a number of pieces being ridiculously big for it. Again, these would have to be stored away until after the sale. The coat stand was hidden under its load. The shelves were laden with books stuffed in any which way, while the fireplace was almost completely hidden. What a waste of a focal point. Not only that, but anyone wanting a country cottage would expect a welcoming fire in the grate and they hadn't finished building the chimney! One of Ken's first jobs was to get up to the roof and rebuild the chimney while I

AFTER

gave the fireplace a much-needed facelift, first cleaning it with a wire brush then polishing it thoroughly. The surround was treated to a stone-look finish with a multi-layered paint effect. The first result was way too wild for the room so we toned it down effectively with an overglaze. All that was then needed was the attention of the local chimney sweep and we could light that fire.

The bookshelves were thinned out and their remaining contents neatly rearranged so they could be seen. The barn had produced a deep cupboard perfect for hiding away the TV. I felt the orange walls would not be to everyone's taste so picked a soft cream instead. Emma was uncertain, worried that it was too similar to the colour of the sofa. I swiftly convinced her that it wouldn't matter in a small space because it would only make it look bigger. And, when it comes to selling your house, bigger is better.

dining

The dining room led off to the right of the living room and was tiny. It looked very squashed but Emma swore they'd had six people 'elbow to elbow' for Christmas dinner. Somehow we had to create some more visual space. This was achieved quite simply by removing a couple of chairs and by repositioning the pictures. I particularly liked the colour scheme they'd chosen so for once we left the walls well alone. With the table laid for four, the room looked inviting and comfortable.

AFTER

Emma
I tend to crowd into spaces if I can

BEFORE

kitchen

Although the units were new, somehow the kitchen didn't gel with the rest of the house. It fell way below the standard set by the other rooms. Ken readily admitted that they'd found it hard to create a theme for the room so they hadn't seemed to mind leaving various jobs undone. I felt that this was probably the room that was hindering the sale most of all. We painted the walls a pretty buttery cream and finished off the units with new handles. A new beech work surface gave a more completed feel to the room, which was helped by boxing in the electricity meter. The mistakes in Ken's last-minute floor job were put right by replacing the uneven and cracked terracotta tiles. My favourite addition was a dual-purpose radiator cover which doubled as a breakfast bar and brilliantly utilised what was otherwise wasted space – unless, of course, we allowed for the dogs' bed, which was out of the question in this case. Everything,

AFTER

including the windows, was thoroughly cleaned until it all looked spotless. I took my lead from the kitchen door when I chose green as the accent colour. Green gingham curtains and blind, a green mat and kitchen accessories all dressed in perfectly to create the feel of a real country kitchen.

AFTER

master bedroom

As downstairs, the furniture in the master bedroom looked as though it belonged to a larger house. Clothes were crammed into the wardrobe and things were stuffed under the bed, giving the impression that there was not nearly enough storage space. That aside, there was nothing attractive in the room, nothing that made it look even remotely inviting. As with the rest of the house, I was able to work with what Ken and Emma already had to make a difference. Thinning out the furniture immediately made the room look bigger. Then we sorted out what was in the wardrobe so that the doors shut, cleared the stuff from under the bed and removed the clothes hanging behind the door. I replaced the tatty rug with a sea grass mat and splashed out on new bedding. Finally, it was a question of dressing in some new fresh strategic items such as the cushions, a new lightshade and some pictures, which all went to lighten up the room and give it that country feeling.

outside

The yard outside the kitchen was something of a disaster area. The view out of the kitchen window was of the ferret cage. It took some persuasion but eventually they were removed to the barn. Both Ken and Emma were extremely unhappy about it

AFTER

Emma

I feel guilty because I sat on the terrace and thought how much I liked it ... I have to keep blocking the ferrets from my mind

but accepted that not everyone would appreciate their pets quite as much as they did. What they had out there was wasted space. Some cane screening and white paint tidied up one wall to define an attractive sitting area. Then Emma and Ken came into their own: Emma did the planting and Ken found some wood features in his workshop, including a table, planter boxes and sculptures. The final touch was the double seat I'd unearthed in their barn and dressed up with a couple of cushions. It hadn't taken much to create a fabulous sitting area where any viewer might imagine sharing an early evening drink or weekend barbecue.

Once we'd finished, Ken and Emma agreed that although there had been moments during the makeover when they had had their doubts, they could see the wisdom behind the changes. The cottage now looked bigger, more traditional and had the benefit of an extra outside room – and no pets. Proof that the treatment worked came only a short time afterwards when they were delighted to accept an offer on the house. They were then able to move into their dream house just up the road.

```
COST
Paint                              £75
Accessories                       £489
  including cream
  double duvet set,
  Roseby's,£54.50
  peeled natural screening,
  Traditional Garden
  Suppliers, £24.95
  cushion covers,
  Henry Newbery & Co Ltd,
  £2.50 each
  'Hove' rug, Ikea, £9
  'Orissa' tiebacks,
  Rufflette, £16.99
Breakfast bar                      £70
Chimney sweep                      £30
Labour                            £230

TOTAL                             £894
```

AFTER
viewers' comments

'It's what you expect in a cottage. It's got that nice welcoming feel to it. I can imagine living here.'

'Before, it was a nice location but the house put you off. Now it's a nice location and a lovely house.'

how to

DISGUISE A BAD VIEW

If you want to retain your privacy or hide a bad view but let light in, avoid net curtains. Use fine fabrics such as muslins, voiles or unlined cotton. They fall well, let light filter through and are attractive. Consider using fabric that will cast a different light into the room and tone with its colour scheme. Antique lace pinned across a window gives a unique effect, but remember that direct sunlight will eventually damage it.

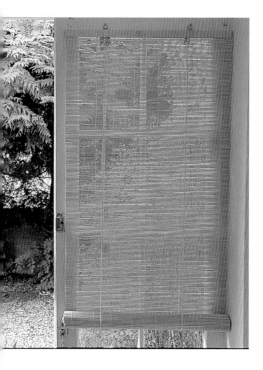

blinds and shutters

Blinds are another good investment. Slatted Venetian blinds come in wood, metal or plastic in different colours and widths. Pulled down, the slats can be angled to control the amount of light flowing into a room. Their only disadvantage is that they can be awkward to clean. Plain roller blinds and Roman blinds can be made with fabrics that filter light and screen an unattractive view. Split-cane and bamboo blinds will add a rather colonial feel and look wonderful with the sun streaming through them.

Vertical louvre blinds are attached to the top and bottom of the window. Usually made of strips of canvas or wood, they pivot open and shut and pull open to the side. Café blinds or curtains cover only the lower half of a window, letting in light above it. Similarly, a type of roller blind can be fitted that rolls up from the bottom of the window. These can be pulled up to the right height to hide the view. Added interest can be given in a bay window by raising adjacent blinds to different heights. Louvred shutters are an alternative. They can be divided so that privacy is retained by only shutting the lower half.

using glass

Glass shelving can be fixed across a window and used to hold plants or ornaments, although this makes opening the window difficult, so ensure that it is not a window that you use often. These shelves will successfully obstruct the view but light will still find its way in around them.

Frosted glass is often used in windows where privacy is particularly desired. If you want the effect without the cost, use a frosting spray. Having cleaned the windows thoroughly, the spray can be used to cover an entire pane or you might stencil a clear line around the edge of the window or patterns in the centre. Frosted film is another possibility. Stuck on to the window, it provides the same effect as frosted glass. For additional interest, or to admit more light, shapes or patterns can be cut out of it.

Churches are not the only preserve of stained or coloured glass. There are modern designs that lend themselves to domestic use. Subtle marbled patterns make a feature of a window while hiding what is behind. Coloured acetate makes a cheap and cheerful alternative. Again, a drawing on tracing paper can be an effective answer. If your room looks on to a brick wall allowing little or no light to come in, paint the wall a bright colour or paint a design or a mural on it to give something interesting to look at.

nifty trick

If little light comes into a basement room, attach an outdoor spotlight to the outside wall and angle it to shine in through the window. If you have covered the window to hide the view, it should look as if the sun has found a way to you after all and will provide more light than there was before.

NEW-LOOK SOFA

Don't show a favourite old sofa the dump. A new loose cover will bring it back to life, making it a welcome part of any new decorative scheme

What you need

- sofa in need of covering
- old sheet or cotton fabric for pattern
- large pins
- fabric marker pen
- scissors
- tape measure
- fabric for finished cover
- matching thread
- fastenings

MAKE PATTERN

To make a loose-fitting sofa cover, you will need to make a pattern first from an old sheet or piece of fabric.

1 Outside arms: Pin the fabric against the outside arm, smoothing it and repinning it so that it is a close fit. With a fabric marker pen, draw the line of the seam. Repeat with the other arm.

2 Outside back: Cut two pattern pieces allowing a 10cm (4in) overlap down the centre. Pin them on to the back of the sofa, folding back the facings for the centre opening. Smooth the fabric out to the side and pin. Draw the seam lines and the centre fold on the fabric, ensuring the two pieces overlap properly. Remove and machine tack the two back seams. Replace the fabric on the sofa.

3 Inside arms: Cut a piece allowing enough fabric to tuck into the side of the sofa and for shaping around the corners. Pin to sofa along the seam line on the outer arm (left). Smooth the fabric over the arm and into the tuck. Mark the seam lines along the arm and down the front edge of the sofa. Push the pen between the seat and the arm to mark the seam line of the tuck-in.

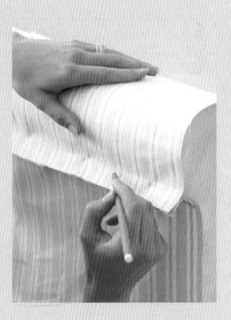

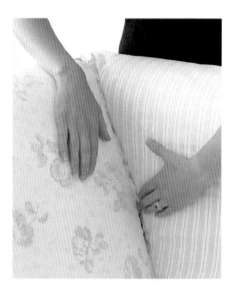

4 Inside back: Cut a section of fabric and pin it to the outside back along the top seam line. Smooth the fabric across the back so that it tucks down into the seat and arms (left). Push the pen into the sides and seat to mark the tuck-in.

5 To get the fabric fitting neatly, make a dart at the top corners of the sofa. Smooth the material towards the corner and cut off the extra (right). Pin the seams, making sure they fit snugly.

6 Unpin the material from the sofa and sew the seams, easing the corner seams by cutting them where necessary. Replace the cover on the sofa to check the fit. Trim off any surplus material and make any adjustments to the seams by remarking and resewing. Cross out the old lines to avoid any muddle.

7 Seat and front skirt: Should be cut as one piece, allowing extra to tuck in at the back and sides of the sofa. Smooth the fabric from the back forwards, pinning in place and marking the seam lines, pushing the pen into the tucks. Pin the sides of the skirt to the arms of the sofa to check the size. Remove and machine tack to the back and arms. Put back on the sofa.

8 Front arms: Cut the fabric and place on the sofa. Smooth and pin from the top downwards (left). Use a dart if necessary. Mark the seams. Repeat for the other arm.

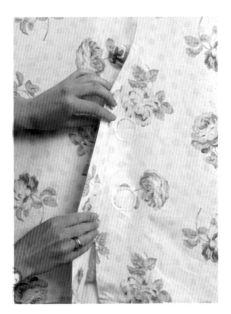

9 Remove the cover from the sofa and machine tack the last seams. Trim the seam allowances to 2cm (¾in). Turn the cover the right side out and replace it on the sofa, working from the front backwards (left). If it doesn't fit anywhere, remark the seams, crossing out the previous lines. Remove and restitch if necessary.

CUT OUT PATTERN

10 Check every seam line is marked. Check every section is marked with its name and that it is clear which is the right side of the fabric. Unpick the cover by cutting along the seam lines. Place the pattern pieces on the furnishing fabric and carefully mark the seam lines, remembering to check the position of any pattern. Cut out the fabric making sure you leave a seam allowance all the way round.

MAKE COVER

11 Follow steps 1–9 again, using the furnishing fabric. Sew the hem by hand and finish the opening at the centre back with velcro, buttons, a zip, loops or ties.

SEAT CUSHIONS

For each seat cushion cut out two pieces of fabric the size of the cushion top plus seam allowances. Cut one long strip the size of three sides plus seam allowances. Cut two pieces the length of one side and half the depth plus seam allowances and sew a zipper between them. Sew the short ends of the strips together, right sides facing. Sew the band to the cushion top, right sides facing. Next, with the zip half open, sew the band to the cushion bottom. Trim the seams, turn the cover the right side out through the zip and insert the cushion.

GLASGOW

One-bedroom ground-
floor flat in imposing
converted stately home.
One reception room with
kitchen; bathroom.
Magnificent location.
£64,000.

Scotland's largest city and one of Europe's cultural capitals, Glasgow boasts numerous museums, art galleries and historical architecture. It's a city of surprising contrasts with its Victorian skyline and Charles Rennie Mackintosh architecture sitting alongside 21st-century attractions such as the Glasgow Science Centre on the Clyde, a thriving café culture and great shopping. In other words, it is a busy cosmopolitan centre with good travel connections with the rest of the UK. The property market has recently gone through the roof with most properties being snapped up within a week of being put up for sale. However, there was one that was proving harder to shift. The one-bedroom apartment in question was in the imposing stately home of Aitkenhead House, surrounded by the tranquillity and open space of Kings Park and only fifteen minutes from the centre of the city. The house had been converted into 14 flats 15 years earlier, all of them highly desirable and immediately snapped up. Eddie had lived happily in his flat until his work as a fire safety officer on nuclear submarines had taken him to Barrow-in-Furness. It was there he had met his fiancée, Julie, and had then decided to sell his bachelor pad to help finance the purchase of a new home for them both: 'I thought it would go quickly. When I saw it, I put an offer in within a couple of days.'

In fact, nobody had shown any interest in the flat in the two months that it had been on the market. Julie thought it might be because it was small and not very nicely decorated but Eddie disagreed 100 per cent. Time for me to make an entrance.

This was a gorgeous location in an historic park and the building took my breath away. As I drove up, I couldn't wait to see inside. But instead of the restrained elegance I was expecting, I was greeted by a place which looked as if no one lived there. The hallway felt gloomy and claustrophobic. The bedroom felt much the same. My heart sank lower with every room we entered, but I saved my ammunition until I saw the living room. I seemed to have wandered into an Egyptian room at the British Museum. Dark red walls were decorated with papyrus prints and large hieroglyphics. Was this the best way to present it to prospective buyers? Like the rest of the flat, the kitchen looked as though it was never used. To give this place even a hope of selling, I had to transform it into the home of luxury and style that matched buyer's expectations from the outside.

> # Julie
> It's small and not very nicely decorated

Doctor's Diagnosis

To introduce life and style we had to:
- Change the colours
- Obliterate the Egyptian motifs
- Add a dining area
- Play up the positive features

BEFORE
viewers' comments

'It was like walking into a high-rise. I was so gutted.'

'Really disappointing. The entrance looks great but once you've been inside, No.'

'It feels awfully claustrophobic and grubby.'

'The bath's filthy and I hate the pea-green colours.'

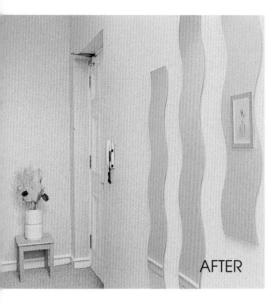

AFTER

entrance

The first two obvious steps to lighten the dark, oppressive hallway involved removing the old carpet and changing the colour of the walls. Sea grass is a wonderful hard-wearing contemporary floorcovering that works well in period homes. I decided to use it throughout the apartment to encourage the feeling that one room flowed into another and to enhance a sense of space. The dull blue walls were painted a parchment colour with white skirting boards and wood trim. Immediately the passageway looked wider. When painting over a dark colour, it's essential to use an undercoat first, especially if the final shade is going to be paler.

   I exchanged the lone pendant light for a smart piece of tracking with several lights that could be angled to illuminate the whole passage more effectively. Another ruse to create the impression of space is, of course, to use mirrors. I used a trio of long wavy-edged ones to reflect the light back into the hallway and give it a slightly modern feel. A picture and a small table with a stylish dried flower arrangement were all it took to complete the transformation – definitely a case of 'less is more'.

BEFORE

bedroom

The bedroom needed work. Nobody in their right mind would sleep in there. The walls were a hideous pea green and the duvet was peculiarly masculine. The 'furniture' consisted of a broken mirror and an unattractive old-fashioned chair. It looked more like a monk's cell than a personal sanctuary. The fact there was no storage space would make buyers question where they would put their belongings. The plus point was the long window but that was ignored and framed by some very tired curtains. Eddie tried to excuse the state of it by claiming it was a blank canvas. Well, if you must leave your buyer a blank canvas, at least make it a clean one. The walls were improved by being painted a soft peach. Then I moved the bed to make better use of the space and made a simple headboard. Textured wallpaper, Lincrusta, was applied to a piece of MDF and then painted silver, a strong contemporary colour. It was repeated in the new bedlinen, contemporary chair and curtains. I chose a pleated blind for the window that pulled upwards to ensure privacy yet allowed in as much light as required. Storage was essential so we made a simple canvas wardrobe to give the idea there was room for something more permanent. As for the poor old plant in the bedroom, I neatly trimmed the partially dead leaves so it didn't look as if it had been hacked to death. With a new lampshade, some cushions for contrast and three small pictures above the bed, it was hard to believe it was the same room. We had created a warm and unisexual look, which should appeal to all buyers.

AFTER

bathroom

The bathroom wasn't the most prepossessing room but it needed only a little attention to turn it into somewhere one might want to spend some private time. It presented a horrible combination of green and pink and looked dated. First, as always,

AFTER

a good clean was in order. The pink melamine cupboards clashed with the green floor but that was easily remedied by using special melamine paint to turn them a cool green. That done, all I needed to do was dress the room with a few light touches. It was out with the tatty shower curtain and in with the new. Following the green theme, some fresh towels, candles and a plant made all the difference, not forgetting the net bag of shells just for fun.

BEFORE

AFTER

living/kitchen

This was the real challenge. As the only living space, it had to be transformed from Eddie's idiosyncratic tribute to things Egyptian into a real selling point. I had decided on a colour scheme for the whole room that centred on one colour. This is a wise move if you have only a small space to work with because it gives a coherent look which won't distract the buyer from the size of the room itself. Eddie was despairing when I revealed my plan. All he could think was beige. All I could see was a principal colour that was elegant and understated and would work with other accents. However, I had to hand it to him as he resigned himself to the task and manfully painted over the red walls with their gold hieroglyphics. As in the other rooms, the old carpet made way for the neutral patterned sea grass. The tatty and smelly green curtains did the long windows no favours. Our budget didn't run to new ones so, after Julie had washed them, I used them as linings for sheer voile curtains. The effect was stunning. Then I rearranged the furniture so it wasn't exclusively focused on the TV and, most importantly, left room for the creation of a small dining area. When selling a property as impressive as this, it's important to remember that the buyer will be buying into a certain lifestyle – and you can bet your bottom dollar it won't include eating a hamburger in front of the TV but something a touch more refined.

Lastly, the kitchen area. Like the bathroom, it needed only a few touches to make a difference. The natural wood trim on the units made them look very 1980s. A lick of white paint and some snazzy new metal handles soon cured that. I always think of handles as jewellery for the kitchen – change them and you change the whole effect. Otherwise we just cleaned until it was gleaming and then dressed in a few simple accessories. Perhaps my favourite touch was adding the silver paint to the wooden room divide. It successfully created a bridge between the two areas.

After all our efforts, the whole apartment had become a modern and inviting place. It looked as though the owner had spent time in it and enjoyed living there. It more than lived up to the expectations set by the superb exterior of the house and its surroundings. To Eddie and Julie's delight, Eddie's company decided to buy the place very shortly afterwards for £1,000 above the asking price.

Eddie
I thought it would be too beige, but I was wrong

COST

Paint	£300
Flooring	£720
Furniture	£137
Accessories	£1,172
Labour	£300
TOTAL	£2,629

AFTER
viewers' comments

'A million times better. It's so much brighter and homely.'

'It's the whole package – a grand exterior with somewhere that looks comfortable to live in.'

'A really different flat. What a transformation.'

PICTURE CREDITS

Thanks to Crown Paints (pages 107 & 108) and the following for their
permission to reproduce the photographs in this book:

Brume
page 133

Chris Ridley
pages 10, 12-16, 24, 26-30, 50, 52-56, 62, 64-69, 74, 76-80,
86, 88-92, 98, 100-104, 124, 126-130, 138, 140-143

Fired Earth
page 83

Hillarys
page 32

Michelle Jones
pages 40-42, 112, 114-117

The Pier
page 44

Pret a vivre
page 35

Robert Harding
pages 22, 23, 36, 37, 46-48, 60, 61, 72, 73, 84, 85, 96, 97, 110,
111, 120-123, 134-137